Forging Healthy
Connections

Praise for Forging Healthy Connections

"We have so much knowledge now—more than enough—to demonstrate to the leaders of the world in all fields—of the overwhelming importance of deep, meaningful relationships in the healthy development of us all, both as individuals and communities. It is time to begin to apply this knowledge— to make it both understandable and usable. Trevor Crow and Maryann Karinch, in their new work, *Forging Healthy Connections*, have done their part well in guiding us to embrace a world where healthy relationships are fostered and supported, so that we may thrive as human beings and live well on this earth."

— Dan Hughes, PhD
Psychologist and author of many books including:
Building the Bonds of Attachment,
Brain-Based Parenting *and*
8 Keys to Building Your Best Relationships

"*Forging Healthy Connections* makes clear the profound impact relationships have on our health and well-being. It is an enlightening journey into a world of possibilities for healing and wellness."

— Ellen Langer
Professor of Psychology, Harvard University,
and author of Mindfulness *and* Counterclockwise

Forging Healthy Connections

*How Relationships Fight Illness,
Aging and Depression*

Trevor Crow, LMFT,
and Maryann Karinch

New Horizon Press
Far Hills, New Jersey

Requests for permission should be addressed to:
New Horizon Press
P. O. Box 669
Far Hills, NJ 07931

Trevor Crow, LMFT, and Maryann Karinch
    Forging Healthy Connections:
    How Relationships Fight Illness, Aging and Depression

Cover design: Charley Nasta
Interior design: Scribe Inc.
Author photo of Trevor Crow courtesy of chrisbaileyphoto.com

Library of Congress Control Number: 2013931894

ISBN 13: 978-0-88282-452-9

New Horizon Press

Manufactured in the U. S. A.

17   16   15   14   13   1   2   3   4   5

AUTHOR'S NOTE

This book is based on the authors' research, personal experiences, interviews and real life experiences. In order to protect privacy, names have been changed and identifying characteristics have been altered except for contributing experts.

For purposes of simplifying usage, the pronouns his/her and s/he are sometimes used interchangeably. The information contained herein is not meant to be a substitute for professional evaluation and therapy with mental health professionals.

Contents

Foreword

The message from the media is that life clicks along in a series of deals. Sadly, it's portrayed as true for our interpersonal relationships as it is for business. We routinely make trades of time, resources and even affection: "If you do this for me, I'll do that for you."

Interpersonal relationships are not only critical to happiness, but also to the effective functioning—that is, the *health*—of individual human beings and organizations of all sizes, from the family to the world. When they become transactional in nature, as they have, we make it nearly impossible for ourselves and our society to enjoy well-being. When deals define a relationship, trouble starts. Not every trade is balanced when it is made. Some things like fidelity, caring, support or the absence thereof can't be easily traded. Treating relationships as transactions distances us from the emotional bonds that enable human connections to thrive.

Relationships are very complicated. They are not bilateral; they take in residue from early childhood and experiences throughout life as well as what we say and do in our daily interactions. When things between us and our loved ones aren't working out, it's easy to forget that complexity. The knee-jerk response for many people to an interpersonal problem is to blame someone—maybe ourselves—for "doing something wrong." For others, it's to ignore the problem. Neither choice is satisfactory. Neither embodies the level of trust that is essential to a healthy connection. The easy answer is often, just get out.

In order to cultivate enduring trust and hopefully fix the problems in our relationships, we need to have compassion for ourselves as well as those with whom we interact. That compassion comes out of understanding what makes us tick. This book gives you the tools to develop that understanding. You will then learn some ways to affect change to strengthen your connections, with the powerful and practical result being that you will *feel better*—in an emotional and a physical sense.

Forging Healthy Connections offers you well-grounded research and stories of successes and failures to help you gain insights into your body, your emotions and your situation. The bad news is there is no magic bullet. Successful relationships require work. The great news is that success is possible.

— Howard H. Stevenson
Professor Emeritus, Harvard University,
and author of *Getting to Giving:*
Fundraising the Entrepreneurial Way

Introduction

We are built for relationships. The need for connection with others permeates the human body.

Emotional bonding profoundly affects the mechanisms inside us that restore health and keep us healthy. The most powerful way to arouse those positive emotions that sustain health and healing is to connect intimately with another human being.

Think about how frightening it is to face a health crisis. Here's an example: One morning, you see a spot on your leg that has changed color and you fear skin cancer. Your left brain kicks in and "helps" you think through the situation. Skin cancer doesn't run in your family. You don't sunbathe or use a tanning bed. When you're in the sun, you don't burn easily. No, this could not be skin cancer.

But that fear stays in your unconscious mind, affecting you throughout the day. You're moody. You don't seem to process information or evaluate options with the same clarity you usually do. If someone asked you, "Are you afraid right now?" you probably would answer, "No," but deep down you might not be so sure.

That evening, your partner comes home and immediately gives you a big hug and kiss. You aren't aware of it, but something starts to happen in your brain. The fog of fear that lurked low and thick in your unconscious mind all day begins to dissipate. You enjoy your dinner and sleep well that night. You wake up in the morning and say to your partner, "I noticed a spot on my leg. I'm going to call the doctor and make an appointment today."

"Good for you, dear," he says. "That's the way to handle it. I'd be happy to go with you."

This simple, ordinary display of caring is exactly the kind of connected behavior that gives the partner's immune system a boost.

In this book, we will share some startling insights and the latest scientific knowledge from experts who document the impact of such caring interactions on human health. The research comes from multiple disciplines, but in studying it, we noticed a convergence of ideas, as well as results that reinforce each other. Neurobiology, psychology, immunology, psychiatry, epigenetics, sociology, radiology—these are just some of the disciplines in which researchers and clinicians state this unequivocally: Positive emotional connections boost our capacity to prevent and combat disease. Their complementary points of view and research can open up a new world of understanding for you about the quality of your relationships, how to improve them and the impact of that improvement on your surviving and thriving.

In Part I we will explore how the body responds to stress, which has a highly destructive effect on health, as well as the relief of stress. The power of stress to affect body systems is so strong that it can affect not only a single person's health, but also the children and grandchildren of that person! In short, if your health is being damaged by stress, multiple generations may suffer as well. Positive connections with others offer the most effective way to reverse that course. Part II will plunge into the myriad ways that society, pop culture and your own family shape your connections and how these things affect your health. Part III will guide you in looking introspectively at your own relationships and, hopefully, making discoveries and showing techniques and strategies that will improve them and help you keep connected.

PART I

Human Nature and Relationships

CHAPTER 1

A Lifelong Necessity

From the moment human beings are born to the moment we die, we need relationships. We get sick, mentally and physically, without the emotional security that flows from positive connections to other beings.

The substance of this book is about connection—need, nature, loss, power and promise—and how this connection must be other-focused as well as self-focused. This is a "we-help" book; it addresses the character and experience of reciprocity. It builds on the reality that the human brain is designed for relationships; it is a social organ. The quality of those relationships, therefore, affects how well the brain itself and the entire organism functions.

The assumption that you are better off pursuing answers to *all* your problems intellectually is ruinous to relationships and to your health. Begin by throwing out that assumption if you hold it. We're falling ill because we don't value our relationships as much as we do our intellectual superiority. We'd rather be proven right instead of being connected to each other. We respect and rely on our ability to think through health problems and minimize the power of emotions to heal.

What we propose about the way you view relationships isn't all that different from a common and highly valued business practice: brainstorming. Commonly, people talk about brainstorming as though it's a purely cognitive exercise, making the process of powering through a problem more intellectually robust. If that's all brainstorming was, then all the participants could go into their separate cubicles, come up with ideas and get the same result as they would in direct conversation. That isn't how it works. The energy generated by sensing others' emotions as they help shape ideas and then drive those ideas from the brain out of the mouth gives the whole experience a sense of movement—right brain to left brain, left to right and so on. Brainstorming is a good example of how superior results—and physical energy—can come from the interplay of emotion and logic.

With this dynamic in mind, think about your relationships. Where's the energy in your relationships if every move you make together is dominated by thinking? How overwhelming would your interaction be if emotion made it hard for you to think? Your relationships represent tremendous possibilities for your well-being when the two come together dynamically.

We need "we-help" more than ever before. We have an ethos of self-focus and disposability, instead of we-focus and durability. The way we fill garbage cans with waste matches the way we may treat an intimate relationship. When we're done with it, we get rid of it. If you're in an abusive relationship, that's a good move, but that's not the case for many people who neglect their relationships or move on just because it seems to take less effort than nourishing them.

Many people, if not most, struggle with how to establish and sustain relationships that are healthy in both the emotional and physical sense of the word. Fear has *no* place in a healthy relationship. The freedom to feel vulnerable is an *essential* part of a healthy relationship. Blaming *never* contributes to the health of any relationship. We will explore all of these elements in the subsequent pages of this book. And in exploring them, it will become clear how fear and blame have corrosive effects on your physical health and how the ability to feel vulnerable is life-giving. Vulnerability is, in fact, a vital ingredient in love.

When interviewed for a *New York Times* article on how his brain imaging studies show the impact of love on the brain, the eminent psychiatrist Daniel J. Siegel stated unequivocally that love promotes physical well-being: "Scientific studies of longevity, medical and mental health, happiness and even wisdom point to supportive relationships as the most robust predictor of these positive attributes in our lives across the life span."[1]

Thoughts to keep in mind as you read this book:

- Medicine is a left-brained discipline; healing is a right-brained process.
- Healthy habits come from choices; physical well-being comes from feelings.
- Stress is vital to self-defense; stress is lethal to health and healing.
- Autonomy is vital for a human being; vulnerability is vital to connecting with another human being.
- Cars are built so they can be fixed; people are built so they can regenerate.

WHAT PART OF YOU RESPONDS TO RELATIONSHIPS?

An experiment known as the "Still Face,"[2] conducted by Edward Tronick, director of the University of Massachusetts Boston's Child Development Unit and co-creator of the Infant-Parent Mental Health Post Graduate Certificate Program, shows the heartbreaking result of a mother severing the connection with her infant *for just two minutes.* The experiment was first conducted in 1975 and was then repeated in 2009. The first scene shows a mother playing happily with her one-year-old baby. The infant smiles, points and clearly interacts with her mother. The mother then turns away; when she faces the baby again, it is with a blank expression. Almost instantly, the baby responds to the difference. She uses all her ability to try to get the mother's attention again, first smiling and pointing, and then trying to reach her with both hands. She resorts to screeching, turning away and sobbing uncontrollably. All the negative responses stop when the mother re-engages with the baby.

In the first part of the experiment, there is a synchronized play of expressions and connections in a relational loop—mommy smiles and baby smiles; baby points and mommy looks where baby is pointing. When we are in that patterned, rhythmic connection with one another, we are laying down positive neurological pathways in our brains. When that's cut off, it's painful. Watch the video to see how much anguish just two minutes of disconnection causes the baby.

The rhythmic response cycle in an adult relationship helps re-inforce certain expectations related to that connection. So when we experience disconnection with our partner, we are like that baby. We may shut our feelings down for a moment, smiling and pointing, and try to cope with the loss. In short, we become avoidant. Alternatively, we might scream for attention. Both are signs of stress that may abate, but will not go away until someone helps us re-establish a sense of emotional equilibrium through a healthy connection.

Tronick explained that this experiment shows the good and the bad but also implies the ugly. The good is the positive, secure interac-tion and the bad is the temporary disruption of it. "The ugly is when you don't give the child any chance to return to the good," he said.[3] People of all ages can experience the bad—and even the ugly—when trust is broken, because without trust we can't sustain connection with other beings. We suffer a persistent sense of being alone.

The implication of the "Still Face" experiment is readily observ-able; it's not a stretch to see the cause-and-effect relationship between connection and joy and denial of connection and anxiety. Research has also documented that we can go several levels deeper than the temporary effect of short-term disconnection from someone we trust. There are physiological levels of meaning suggested by this experi-ment, with effects that are not as clearly defined and observable as a sobbing, distressed infant.

Epigenetics is an emerging science that explores the way human interaction with the environment affects the functioning of our DNA and produces inheritable traits. The genes themselves don't change, but people close to us and circumstances around us affect the expres-sion of our genes. That change in expression is what is inherited.

In 2011, research-psychologists Kathryn Gudsnuk and Frances Champagne, from Columbia University, published their findings on the "Epigenetic effects of early developmental experiences."[4] Their work demonstrates how trauma during early stages of growth can affect brain development and behavior. Epigenetic mechanisms play a key role in shaping our biology in response to factors in the environment—the stress of war, the feeling of fear and isolation from being orphaned and so on. Such findings in research suggest that "prenatal maternal stress, postnatal maternal care, and infant neglect/abuse can lead to epigenetic variation"[5] and those factors may have long-term effects on behavior, stress responses and brain plasticity (the lifelong ability of the brain to adjust neural pathways based on new experiences).

Our bodies respond to connection and the lack of it on the most superficial level all the way down to the most fundamental one. We sob and swear when someone we trust lets us down; we laugh and hug when trust is upheld and the connection feels strong. But we don't simply display responses; in fact, responding to connections or the lack of them goes even deeper than our cells. Our bodies take action on a genetic level that not only affects us, but it also affects our offspring and, ultimately, our family line. When we help ourselves heal and stay strong through connections, we affect the health and well-being of generations to come.

HOW DO YOU CONNECT WITH OTHERS?

The early experiences that shape our brain circuits and affect our genes lead to strategies in the way we bond with others.

Psychologist John Bowlby's seminal work in this area explored how the nature of our attachment to others is hard-wired and affects our relationships throughout our lives. From an early age, Bowlby had personal reasons that drove his curiosity about attachment: He grew up in a household in Great Britain where his mother spent very little time with him, so his "mother" was his nanny. And then at the age of seven, his parents sent him to boarding school. In other words, his early years might be described as a series of attachment challenges.

In 1950, Bowlby undertook a project for the World Health Organization to study the mental health of homeless children. The resultant report delivered substantial insights about the need for mother-child attachment and ways to safeguard it, but he felt it had a "grave limitation. Whereas it had much to say about the many kinds of ill effects that evidence shows can be attributed to maternal deprivation and also about practical measures that may prevent or mitigate these ill effects, it said very little indeed about the processes whereby these ill effects are brought into being."[6] That realization set Bowlby on a course of research that led to his 1969 book *Attachment and Loss*, which established him as the father of attachment theory. He concluded that our attachment styles not only have their roots in the infant-caregiver relationship, but that they also have a genetic and evolutionary component that aids in our survival.

To understand how attachment theory functions in your own life, consider both the characteristics and styles of attachment.

CHARACTERISTICS OF ATTACHMENT

Bowlby described distinguishing characteristics of attachment that can be summarized as *proximity maintenance, safe haven, secure base* and *separation distress*.

In introducing proximity maintenance, Bowlby says, "at some stage in the development of the behavioural systems responsible for attachment, proximity to mother becomes a set-goal."[7] To make the application lifelong, we can express this characteristic as a desire to be close to people we're attached to. Safe haven means coming back to those we're attached to when we need security and comfort, for example, in the face of a threat. Secure base is like a human shark cage: a reliable source of safety that allows a person to explore a potentially dangerous environment without getting hurt. Separation distress is the anxiety a person feels when the attachment figure is gone.

STYLES OF ATTACHMENT

For decades, the discussion of attachment in professional literature focused on human babies, monkey babies, baboon babies and so on. Mary Ainsworth, who worked with John Bowlby, developed a classic experiment in 1978 called the Strange Situation Study, in which young children played with their mother or some other caregiver to whom they were very attached, then were briefly left alone with a stranger and then reunited with the mother. Out of that came her classification of attachment styles: *secure, ambivalent-insecure* and *avoidant-insecure* attachment.[8] A few years later, researchers added a fourth attachment style known as *disorganized-insecure*.[9]

In the 1980s, experts started to talk more about attachment in relation to adults. Basing their work on Ainsworth's, psychologists Cindy Hazen and Philip Shaver connected the idea of attachment to romantic love.[10] Their categories of styles roughly corresponded to the four applying to infants.

Styles of attachment in adulthood are the same as in childhood; they just have different names. The child who avoids attachment would be the adult who is dismissive. The child who is ambivalent about attachment is the adult who is preoccupied (chaotic). The secure kid is the autonomous adult—someone who has the ability to regulate himself alone or with the attachment figure. The disorganized-insecure child is the fearful (anxious) adult. We will use the terms in parentheses to describe the attachment styles because they are the ones commonly used in family therapy and couples' counseling.

A diagram available on the web illustrates the different types using characters from the cartoon strip *Peanuts*. Peppermint Patty was secure or autonomous, Lucy van Pelt was preoccupied, Schroeder was dismissive and Charlie Brown was fearful. Although Charles Schultz created enduring personalities in his strip, here are a few twenty-first century examples to clarify the types:

- The adult with secure attachment knows how to balance autonomy needs with relationship needs. This is not to say that "secure" equates to "perfect" in a relationship! Securely-attached people can also have unresolved issues.

- The chaotically-attached adult relies way too much on other people and has a disorganized, or chaotic, way of relating to others. In a relationship with someone who's chaotic (preoccupied), you would get a sense of "come to me; go away," with the person asking for attention, and then dismissing it.

- The adult with an avoidant attachment style relies far too much on himself. If someone he cares for walks out on him, then recants and comes back, he would not welcome her back with open arms. He is much more likely to turn around (figuratively and literally) and avoid the person.

- The anxiously-attached adult would have a great deal of difficulty "co-regulating," that is, reciprocally experiencing a calming effect by connecting with another person.

| Secure | Chaotic (Preoccupied) | Avoidant (Dismissive) | Anxious (Fearful) |

The autonomously-attached is very good at balancing emotion with thinking or reflecting so they can integrate thoughts and feelings, whereas the avoidantly-attached person tends to be far too cognitive and can't allow emotions to guide thinking. In contrast, the anxiously-attached person is too emotional. Since emotions and thinking work best together, one of these latter attachment styles can lead to interpersonal difficulties at work and at home.

SECURE VERSUS AVOIDANT VERSUS ANXIOUS IN THE WORKPLACE

Vinny Mullineaux is the CEO of Vertrax, a logistics solutions company for the oil, gas and propane industry. Vertrax's software helps oil and gas companies plan, track and bill oil deliveries in real time. The company is best known for a game-inspired tablet that the drivers find fun and easy to use.

Mullineaux's engineers come from around the globe: India, Pakistan, Russia, Malaysia, Thailand and the United States, and they all work together in teams on tasks. Rather than have a hierarchical organization structure, Mullineaux established a flat structure with team/task oriented groups. In one group, for example, he might be working on developing content for part of a website, and the team leader may have to ask him to speed up and complete his portion of the task. This flattened team process allows young engineers the opportunity to lead while tapping into their talent as coders. It leads to greater output and creativity leading to more adaptability within the industry.

His mantra—"True power is being able to give it away"—describes his day-to-day functioning, so we would describe his leadership style as secure. Mullineaux doesn't need or want to control each step of the creative process. He is comfortable with being on a team and allowing another engineer to "drive the bus."

An avoidantly-attached or dismissive leader would need the security of an organizational chart and would not be able to emotionally support the team while being task/time oriented in a "top down" way.

Jack Price, the former head of a major information technology trade association based in Washington, DC, was exactly this kind of avoidantly-attached leader. Preceded by an executive vice president with a secure attachment style, Price decided to differentiate himself by bringing his military orientation to the workplace. He began his reign by calling a staff meeting in which an organizational chart clearly stating everyone's "rank" dominated the discussion of how things were about to change. That set the tone for the group, which soon developed a shocking attrition rate.

As a military leader, Price had excelled. His life exemplified the kind of discipline that the military rewards and expects a senior officer to enforce. Along with that ability came interpersonal blind spots, however. He was hard on himself and typically didn't recognize his own emotional needs or stresses—he had no compassion for himself—so he rarely recognized anyone else's needs. In times of crisis, whether personal as in a health issue or something like a natural disaster affecting an entire community, he did not respond with empathy. He suppressed his own feelings so consistently that he had no sensitivity regarding others' emotional reactions to trauma. Price's answer to a tough situation was a "suck it up" speech. His behavior made others want to avoid him.

Steve Jobs was a leader with an anxious attachment style and would be called a "pursuer" in a relationship. (This is covered in greater depth in later chapters.) According to those around him, well documented in sources such as Walter Isaacson's bestselling biography, the Apple founder was anxious, insecure, controlling, critical and blaming. The behavior Isaacson describes is that of someone who is in touch with emotions rather than dismissive of them, but feeling his own anxiety so strongly that it robs him of the ability to feel what other people are feeling:

> Was Jobs's unfiltered behavior caused by a lack of emotional sensitivity? No. Almost the opposite. He was very emotionally attuned, able to read people and know their psychological strengths and vulnerabilities. He could stun an unsuspecting victim with an emotional towel-snap, perfectly aimed. He intuitively knew when someone was faking it or truly knew something. This made him masterful at cajoling, stroking, persuading, flattering, and intimidating people.[11]

Anxiety is a fear response, so the sympathetic nervous system is keyed up. It's very difficult to co-regulate in that state, to take in other people's experiences and be empathetic toward them or to respond to their caring, giving behavior. This state, as well as its deleterious effects on health, will be covered in chapter 3.

As much as you may have the urge to criticize one type or applaud another, consider that these attachment styles were not choices made by these individuals. They took shape because of their own early experiences and the styles and experiences of their early caregivers.

But attachment styles are not rigid; you aren't stuck with a style just because of your parents. It is possible to reconfigure your attachment styles, although it's important to note that they are not fluid.

Even though we can change, the odds are that if you had one classification of attachment as a child, you'd be in the parallel classification as an adult. You can certainly go towards security or organization or you can go in the opposite direction, but the style will not change overnight, nor are you likely to change styles throughout your life. As the result of trauma, you may move away from the secure attachment you developed as a child with your loving parents. Or, you may start out with ambivalent, dismissive or disorganized attachment as a kid and, as an adult, you have the good fortune of good relationships with the people close to you who followed your parents. Perhaps mentors, relatives, friends or a partner stepped in. You can change based on those relationships.

Under stress, a person may fall back on an old attachment style. She may have to rely on others to resurrect and maintain the new, adult attachment style after a job loss, divorce or serious illness, for example. The reversion doesn't signal a total about-face; however, it can temporarily disrupt connections that had seemed great.

Since we're human beings, we are also full of exceptions to rules and live in defiance of classifications. This is true with attachment styles as well. It's possible to have an attachment style *most of the time* but not always. You may be classified as "secure," yet are unresolved around a particular issue or theme. Perhaps your father had a way of trying to show affection for you that you found demeaning and your partner occasionally does something that reminds you of it. He may trigger an avoidant or anxious response, even though the relationship is solid and healthy. Because you are unresolved about the issue, you are suddenly not secure.

WHAT DOES CONNECTING MEAN TO YOUR SURVIVAL?

If you have connected, secure relationships, your immune system is stronger, your health is better and you will recuperate faster from whatever health issues you might have. People have emotional connections to sports teams—you may be a Red Sox fan or a Yankees fan (never both). This is a common example of how we strive to attach to others throughout our lives and it's something we *need* to do on the deepest level of our humanity.

Immunologist D. Kim Burnham, a professor of microbiology and molecular genetics at Oklahoma State University, has written extensively about this link between tribal connections and immunity. He asserts:

> *"Despite the tendency of immunity in vertebrates to focus on the survival of the individual, there is still a significant social component to the immune system in higher animals and people. Pregnant women share their antibodies with their unborn babies during pregnancy and then after birth in breast milk. Likewise, products of the immune system try to get us from sharing our germs with others by making us tired, sleepy and irritable so that we will reduce our contact with others.*
>
> *"In the animal kingdom, even slight decreases in heart function and immunity can be very dangerous to the point that these impairments could likely weed out the antisocial by contributing to an early death. Likewise, slight boosts in immunity due to the benefits of sociality are the ticket to survival.*[12]

Consider what Burnham asserts in light of this essay we received from Peter Edelstein, oncologist, award-winning medical educator and author of an upcoming book for cancer patients called *Own Your Cancer*. When he heard we were writing this book, he wanted to contribute his ideas on the immense healing power of intimate relationships that he has observed with cancer patients:

> *I have been privileged in my role as a surgeon not only to provide medical care to numerous cancer patients, but also to partner with these individuals and, often, with their loved ones as they travel on the overwhelming journey that is cancer. As a witness to survival and loss, optimism and forfeit, and countless other emotions and events that make up the cancer experience, I have received an education far more profound than that I attained in the classroom.*
>
> *From a purely scientific perspective, there continues to be disagreement (often strong disagreement) on the impact (if any) of a cancer patient's loving family relationships (or lack thereof) on that patient's disease course (including the ultimate outcome). An analytical critique of this medical debate is outside the scope of this work. However, my significant real-world clinical experiences have shaped my own personal views on the role that a patient's personal relationships, particularly the deeply intimate love shared with family, play in the life of those with cancer.*
>
> *It is no surprise that relationships with other people often motivate cancer patients to 'do better' by encouraging compliance with the recommended treatment plan. This observation is not, of course, unique to individuals suffering from cancer. My daughters "do better" in school because of their relationship with me (I push them, or as they would describe it, 'nag' or 'annoy'). Want to really use your gym membership? Commit to your best friend to meet three days*

a week at 6 A.M. for a shared workout. Otherwise, your membership card will simply gather dust in your underwear drawer. Given the significant disincentives associated with, say, chemotherapy (severe nausea, followed by dizziness and fatigue, followed by severe nausea and repeat), strong motivation is often required to keep the cancer patient moving along their treatment plan. But while this form of motivation is extremely impactful (it increases the likelihood that the cancer patient will "do better"), the relationship on which the impact is founded can be deep (a loving spouse) or superficial (a home health nurse). Fortunately, most cancer patients have relationships which favorably impact their motivation.

There is, however, another relationship-based impact that I have witnessed much less frequently and is much more empowering. I've caught it in a momentary shared look or in a touch of that uniquely special someone's hand upon the patient's hand. Seemingly small things trigger from deep within the cancer patient a formidable inner strength, peace, calmness and hope. I've witnessed enormously powerful feelings that can only be elicited by a specific individual with whom the patient shares a rare, consuming and intimate love. From such a deep, loving relationship, be it with a spouse, a sibling or a child, pours forth not only the reason, but also the means to survive and to live.

Okay, sometimes Hollywood doesn't exaggerate, and I have been surprised (even amazed) to see real life contradict everything that I know academically and objectively should occur. To watch as a cancer patient who clearly should be dead or near death survives "as promised" to a husband or a wife, a child or grandchild, in order to share in an event of great personal meaning. To still be alive and with adequate mental faculties to appreciate the graduation of a son, the birth of a grandchild, their [last] wedding anniversary. An event with enormous significance to the

*patient, because it is of enormous significance to someone
with whom the patient has that truly loving relationship,
is what drives this medically unexpected survival. Now,
don't get me wrong: I've also partnered with patients who
did not survive to see that graduation or birthday. Clearly
much depends on the type and stage of their cancer. But I
have known them, patients who find the strength and peace
and capacity born of that rare, loving relationship which
empowers them to reach a milestone before they die.*

*More often than a surprising length of life, I have ob-
served the dramatic impact of such intense loving relationships on my patients' quality of life. What can explain how
at times a cancer patient, a person who should likely be at
his or her lowest point in life, facing uncertainty at best and
death at worst, seems to find great peace, joy and happiness? No doubt for some patients their diagnoses serve as
'wake-up calls,' alerting them, reminding them, emphasizing
to them not only how precious life is, but how 'for granted'
we often take those parts of our life that make it so. But
there is more to this phenomenon than that, something else
which allows some who harbor cancer to experience true
happiness. The recognition and appreciation of the routine
little things that envelop our treasured relationships make
life the gift that it is: waking up next to your wife, watching
your grandchildren playing tag on the lawn, agonizing with
your dad over a football game. It is encompassing peace,
calm, strength and appreciation that a small and fortunate
group of men and women unfortunately stricken with cancer receive from their profoundly powerful loving relationships that allow them to feel "more alive" than ever before
despite their cancer.*

In an April 2009 article in *The New York Times*, Tara Parker-Pope,
reporter and author of multiple books on health issues, explored the
same issue as Burnham and Edelstein from a different angle. She noted:

*Researchers are only now starting to pay attention to the
importance of friendship and social networks in overall
health. A [ten-year] Australian study found that older
people with a large circle of friends were 22 percent less
likely to die during the study period than those with fewer
friends. A large 2007 study showed an increase of nearly
60 percent in the risk for obesity among people whose
friends gained weight. And last year [2008], Harvard
researchers reported that strong social ties could promote
brain health as we age.*[13]

There is a flip side to this as well. Social pain, which would include a damaged or severed connection with a loved one, has been linked to actual pain and severe health consequences. In her book on heart health, Dr. Suzanne Steinbaum, director of Women and Heart Disease at the Heart and Vascular Institute of Lenox Hill Hospital in New York, describes a potentially fatal condition called Takotsubo's cardiomyopathy—broken heart syndrome.[14] It results from chronic stress after an emotional shock or trauma. Stress hormones surge (a potentially deadly occurrence explored further in chapter 3), which sends the heart rate and blood pressure skyrocketing. The heart is on overload and stops functioning. The key thing to note is that it is not anything like a conventional heart attack in which the arteries are blocked. In this case, the arteries are normal. Studies on the effects of grief on the body affirm this. According to the Sudden Cardiac Arrest Association, people who have just lost a loved one are twenty-one times more likely to have a heart attack within one day of the death.[15]

Rejection can cause social *and* physical pain. In their study "Why Does Social Exclusion Hurt? The Relationship Between Social and Physical Pain," psychologists Geoff MacDonald of the University of Queensland and Mark R. Leary of Wake Forest University explain how this happens. The conundrum to them was that physical pain and social pain come from two different sets of stimuli (physical from touch and social from sights and sounds), so how could they end up being processed the same way? Yet, the fact is, the human brain can process and experience these different types of signals as though they were from the same source and there are implications for chronic disorders.[16]

Tara-Pope pursued the theme of intimate relationships again in her article "Is Marriage Good for your Health?" She referred to studies that have documented that married people—which could also mean partners in a loving relationship—are less likely to get pneumonia, have surgery, develop cancer or have heart attacks.[17] Psychiatrist Janice Kiecolt-Glaser, in conjunction with her colleagues in behavioral medicine and psychology at Ohio State University, closely studied the correlation between marital status, health and immune function. She makes powerful statements related to those studies:

> *"Marital relationships are strongly related to many aspects of physical health. Not only are married individuals healthier than single, divorced or separated and widowed individuals after controlling for income and age; marital status has substantial predictive power for mortality from a range of chronic and acute conditions. Compared to other social relationships, marital relationships tend to have a greater impact on an individual's emotional and physical well-being. Indeed, a meta-analysis of autonomic, endocrine, and immune data suggests that family relationships, including marriage, are particularly important."*[18]

One of the memorable stories Trevor was told in studying to become a therapist involved residents accompanying a cardiac surgeon on Grand Rounds. The surgeon pointed to two men in rooms across the hall from each other. Both had just had heart surgery and they had similar backgrounds in terms of socio-economic, age, race and health issues. He posed the question to the residents: "Who is more likely to survive this dramatic health event?" One of the residents noticed that cards, flowers and balloons filled one man's room, while the other's had none of those. She correctly identified the man with the expressions of caring as the one who was more likely to survive.

Susan and Jake had been married for four months when he was diagnosed with an advanced case of lung cancer and given less than six months to live. Five years later, he is still alive. We should note that he has access to the best medical care that money can provide. Despite that same access, many patients facing Jake's prognosis give in, give up and die in accordance with the doctors' predictions. In this case, Susan fought the disease alongside him; she provided practical support every day with such joy and generous spirit that his immune system strengthened. He kept active and optimistic. Jake still has the disease and he still fights it every day. And any realist would add that, despite the near-miracle he has already experienced, he probably won't make it to old age.

If you knew that love could give you an "extra" five or six years, though, would you give it a try?

Trevor's stepfather and the author of the foreword for this book, Howard Stevenson, had a massive heart attack—a so-called widow-maker heart attack. The survival rate is miniscule because treatment must occur within the tiny window of ten to twenty minutes. Howard happened to be in front of a building at Harvard Business School, where he is on the faculty, and someone who had just taken a CPR class saw him fall to the ground. The man immediately grabbed the automated external defibrillator (AED) in the building and began working on Howard. At that moment, an ambulance was passing on the bridge over the Charles River, going in the direction of the hospital. Within forty-five minutes of the event, stents were being implanted in Howard's chest. One result of this event was *Howard's Gift: Uncommon Wisdom to Inspire Your Life's Work* (St. Martin's, 2012); the other was an even stronger appreciation for his relationship with his wife, Trevor's mother, who is a cancer survivor.

Trevor believes that neither of them would have survived what they experienced without the other. The good fortune of excellent, prompt medical care counts for a lot; however, it is not 100 percent of the story in a recovery.

Does that healing connection always need to be experienced with a spouse, partner, child or best friend? Not necessarily. We can experience profound connection with professional caregivers, as well as our cats and dogs. After the massacre of twenty children and six adults at Sandy Hook Elementary School in Newtown, CT, on December 14, 2012, Lutheran Church Charities brought eight therapy dogs to help comfort the survivors at the school. The Golden Retrievers had more than a calming effect on both children and adults: In some instances, their presence and unconditional affection facilitated true healing. One little girl who had been in the midst of the rampage started talking to one of the dogs as she was petting it. They were the first words she had spoken in the three days since the shooting.[19]

Maryann's friend Kate had a psychotherapist who expressed sincere caring for her—in a professional manner—while Kate was going through treatments for lung cancer. Without knowing it, the therapist followed a protocol that Dr. Daniel A. Hughes (*Attachment-Focused Therapy*) named PLACE. Hughes, well-known for his work in attachment therapy, began with PACE—playfulness, acceptance, curiosity and empathy—and then added an "L" for love.[20] Like Jake, described earlier, Kate surpassed life-expectancy predictions. She did pass away eventually, but her extra moments of life felt rich and precious.

The first element of Hughes's therapy is vital in both mental and physical healing. The "play" part of PLACE gives people a break after they do good work and helps them to relax. It conveys optimism. You aren't going to be playful if you think a situation is hopeless. It also helps to illuminate humanity more, getting the person to display a part of himself that is not stuck in problems. This is not a matter of a therapist inserting jokes just to generate laughter, but rather a natural part of conversing that may involve lighthearted comments—just to see another perspective on a situation that might be very challenging. Patients feel more optimistic after they experience the "P."

The commonalities that all of these people shared, both the sick and the caregivers, are a heart connection and a deep sense of gratitude for that connection. The evidence is more than anecdotal. In addition to the studies previously referenced above in the Parker-Pope *New York Times* articles and the work of Kiecolt-Glaser, one study conducted by Kathleen B. King, PhD, RN, professor emeritus in the

School of Nursing at the University of Rochester in New York, concluded: "Overall, people who were married when they had coronary artery bypass surgery were 2.5 times more likely to be alive fifteen years later than unmarried people, and the happily married fared better than those in unhappy marriages."[21]

MIND-BODY OR BODY-MIND?

The concept of a mind-body connection can involve techniques by which a person uses the mind to affect the body. For example, some people meditate to slow down their breathing and heart rate and move into a state of deep relaxation. Some people use hypnosis to help them eliminate an addiction or counter pain so they can undergo surgery without anesthesia. Therapies in which thinking precedes emotional engagement in a health issue are extensions of applying this approach to the relationship of mind and body. Another way to look at the impact of mind on body is broken heart syndrome: The arteries are fine, but the heart attack occurs nonetheless.

To some prominent people in the psychiatric community of the late nineteenth and early twentieth centuries, mind-body connection meant something quite different. Their focus was on the body affecting the mind.

This perception of mind-body connection reflected a belief in pyrotherapy—fever therapy—for which Austrian psychiatrist Julius Wagner-Jauregg earned a Nobel Prize in 1927. His concept took shape after observing that his mentally ill patients at the Vienna Asylum who contracted diseases like tuberculosis and typhoid, which involved high fevers, seemed much more in control and lucid while they were sick. Their depression, mania, paranoia or other mental issues abated. Wagner-Jauregg then did something that modern researchers would find appalling. He injected some of his patients with an extract of tubercle bacteria to see what would happen. Fever hit and they got better! Excited at the prospect of curing people at the asylum, he induced a more intense fever than that associated with the bacteria by injecting his patients with malaria. Other physicians followed his lead, initially with encouraging results. Unfortunately, when the fever went away, so did the benefits. Some critics were quick to point out that the malaria killed a few of these patients, so perhaps this wasn't a reliable long-term solution to mental illness.

In his book *Infectious Behavior*, Paul H. Patterson describes a situation much like dreamers looking at the moon, seeing "holes" and thinking it was made of Swiss cheese: "The papers of that era suggest that the investigators were focused on the microbes that caused infection rather than on the immune system's responses to those microbes."[22]

From this early work came two giant questions:

1) Is it possible that the immune system's functioning actually sustains mental illness, and that disrupting it with a disease like malaria counters that effect? In this scenario, fever is seen as a symptom of a disease.

2) Is it possible that a super-charged immune system is exactly what's needed to counter depression, paranoia and so on? In this scenario, fever is an indication of the immune system in "fight" mode.

The common element in the two views is the immune system. We will explore further the effect of human connection—positive and negative—on the immune system and the reciprocity between mind and body in upcoming chapters.

CHAPTER 2

A Full-Bodied Experience

Emotion originates and is experienced throughout the body. In contrast, it's common to think of emotion as something that emanates from one portion of the brain and then affects the body. That view limits a person's ability to understand why attachments are truly full-bodied experiences.

It may be useful at times to make a shift in the way we think of emotion—at least for a moment. What if emotion took on the character of a verb, as psychiatrist Daniel Siegel suggests in his essay "Emotion as Integration: A Possible Answer to the Question, What is Emotion?":

> *Emotion is not a noun, but rather a verb. It may be useful to sit with this thought that emotion is a verb for a moment. Emotion-related words and concepts are active processes, not fixed entities. Seeing emotion as a verb opens our mind to a fluid, moving mechanism that acts, changes, transforms.*[1]

Whether or not we accept this verb approach to the word "emotion," people in the psychology field can't seem to agree on a definition of it. We see it in action and use it as a therapeutic element, but defining it is like grabbing a snowflake: "I've got it! No, I don't!" Siegel comes as close as anyone to being able to grab the snowflake and stop with, "I've got it!" He considers emotion as a shift in the state of integration.

Thinking of words synonymous with integration might help in deepening an understanding of what he is saying; words such as "assimilation" and "absorption," which convey strong senses of taking in something and having it become a part of you. A shift in that state could mean that you are *not* taking in something and/or you take it in but it does not change you. A shift in that state could also mean you are taking in something *more efficiently*, or making better use of it once you take it in. What if that "something" is the healing power of love? Emotion, then, can be seen as the action that takes love in and makes it work or blocks love's entry into you.

INTERNAL AND EXTERNAL SIGNS

Consider first, from both an internal and an external perspective, how emotion drives processes throughout the human body.

Think of a moment of intense anticipation in your life. Trevor was a competitive figure skater, so one of those moments for her was just before beginning a winning routine when she was twelve, with all eyes on her and the music about to start. For Maryann, it was the second before she made her entrance in the starring role of her high school play, *Pygmalion*. For many men and women, it's just before they utter the words "I do" on their wedding days. We have several moments of intense anticipation in our lives and we have the sensation that the universe preserves these moments more clearly for us than ordinary slices of time—like a cosmic snapshot.

To a less noticeable degree, this full-bodied experience of emotion happens all the time. You're driving your car at the speed limit through town. A police siren suddenly pierces the music that you're listening to on the radio. Your mind races to the question, *Is he after me?* Even though you know you haven't done anything to get pulled over, your pulse still quickens. But pulse rate isn't a standalone biological occurrence; if your pulse rate speeds up, then there's involvement of your respiratory system, metabolism and so on. It's reminiscent of the song "Dry Bones":

> *Well, your toe bone connected to your foot bone,*
> *Your foot bone connected to your heel bone,*
> *Your heel bone connected to your ankle bone...*[2]

Reading body language provides an external perspective on how emotion has invasive physical effects. The way a person acts and talks when at ease, or "in neutral," is called that person's baseline.[3] Emotion causes a deviation from the baseline, so reading body language involves seeing how that emotion surfaces. It could show up as a nervous gesture that may have the appearance of grooming, like straightening a necklace or stroking one's neck. Or it could cause the person to move her eyes in a different direction or angle the body away from the source of discomfort.

A young woman is seated on the subway on her way to work. She has her computer tablet in hand and is playing a game. A very handsome man sits down next to her and, with an engaging smile, asks, "Are you winning?" She gently rakes her fingers through her hair, pulls the face of the tablet to her chest and giggles, "No." She is a little nervous and excited by the attention from this man she considers attractive.

All of us, like that young woman, give away our emotional secrets through body language. Most of us don't pay attention to those deviations from baseline, however, and even if we did, we might not know how to identify the emotions behind the body language.

At the same time we have a cognitive sense of love, appreciation, disgust, anger and other emotional states, they also can affect our muscle tension, heart rate, pupil dilation, tone of voice and much more. Awareness is the tip of the iceberg; the effect of those emotions on our body is the greater part of the iceberg. We delve into this physiological impact more deeply in chapter 3, which explores the fight-flight-freeze responses to any threat—physical, psychological or emotional.

EMOTION, PSYCHOTHERAPY
AND CHANGE

Jeremy D. Safran and Leslie S. Greenberg's 1991 book, *Emotion, Psychotherapy and Change*, discusses cultivating an understanding of how emotions originate throughout the body.

Their aim was "to map the various ways that emotion influences the change process" as it pertains to psychotherapy.[4] One of the first things they point out is how lame and general the traditional terms were for describing the role of emotion in therapy. Therapists would speak in terms of emotional insights and catharsis, which didn't help patients develop a specific way of talking about how they felt and what part of them seemed to be giving rise to an emotion. The researchers also had come to see emotions "as an orienting system that provides the organism with adaptive information."[5]

Like the example of the police siren blaring behind your car, you experience the emotion of fear throughout your body before your cognitive brain kicks in and tells you to calm down. Even knowing that, most people would probably explain their reaction by saying, "I thought he was after *me*." In fact, it's just the opposite, with the emotions taking the lead in adapting to the situation. Trevor sees couples all the time who explain their responses to their partner's caring touch by saying, "I know I love him when he holds my hand." Actually, you feel love throughout your body and then your brain wakes up and sends the message, "I know I love him."

The people who contributed to Safran and Greenberg's research inspired many of us not only to honor the importance of emotions in healing and disease, but also to use a multi-disciplinary approach to *prove* the importance of them. We sought—and found—more than observed evidence of emotionally-related therapies working thanks to studies in fields such as neurobiology, psychology, sociology and epigenetics. We came to understand that you cannot think away mental and/or physical health problems or that the sheer force of your will and logic will give you continued health. You need relationships—healthy attachments—and that means you need to be close to your emotions.

Drawing from this emotion-oriented work, Diana Fosha pioneered a way to help patients overcome traumatic and challenging emotional experiences. Her contributions to understanding how and why people heal have relevance for anyone, not just victims of trauma.

Fosha's treatment model is called Accelerated Experiential Dynamic Psychotherapy (AEDP).[6] In contrast to approaches that begin with having the patient come up with compelling reasons to change and thinking through issues as a path to healing, Fosha's approach suggests that thinking and deciding never come first. Her fundamental premise is:

> *"...there's a healing force, drive —a drive or a motivation—to heal and to grow and toward self-repair—that's operating in every single individual, no matter what history of trauma or suffering they have had.*
>
> *"And one of the key aspects of this approach is to assume that, from the get-go, that kind of healing drive is in operation; that healing is not only something that the therapist is going to try to bring about as an outcome, but that it's something that resides within the person, and it's something to be activated from the get-go.*
>
> *"And I guess the other...is that it's an attachment-based model, and that we really understand the nature of emotional difficulties as developing in the context of aloneness—and actually, unwilling, unwanted aloneness..."*[7]

Flip this theory around and you get "the nature of emotional health develops in the context of connection." This thought captures the heart of Fosha's therapeutic system: the creation of a safe relationship is attached to the work with the therapist. The bonds established with the therapist allow the victim of trauma to experience emotions without fear. They can find a place of healing because they are looking for someone who provides safe haven. All of this happens within the bounds of the secure therapist-client relationship.

AEDP is an approach to helping people heal through bottom-up processing: first being able to identify the emotion and then describing what it does to them physically. The power of this approach is just as valid with people going through a rough spot in their marriage as it is for the victim of childhood abuse.

Our culture has not nurtured our development of a toolkit to sense what's happening with our bodies or to describe how we feel. Commonly, people talk around issues and emotions by listing symptoms, which generally begins as a litany of what someone else did to us.

Let's say you've just come in for your first session and Trevor asks you what's going on for you; how do you feel? You respond by telling her about how your partner picks on you and criticizes everything you do and never appreciates you. It may take time before she asks you the same questions and you finally say, "I'm angry." But even that doesn't tell her much of anything. "Angry" comes from somewhere, just like methane gas comes from somewhere. It's an indication of something that occurred before, and not just some unkind words from your partner. It goes back to sensitivities and barriers you developed growing up in your family of origin. Talking about those formative experiences and how they make us feel is a new process for most of us.

We have to learn about our own felt sense of what is happening in the moment—to be in the moment and emotionally available. As we mentioned above, Trevor has sat in therapy with men and women who enjoy the touch of their partners and then conclude that the origin of their positive feelings is a cognitive process. Part of the problem is that they honestly cannot describe what they feel when the people they love hold their hands. Trevor even had one client who knitted his brow when she asked him how it made him feel and he said, "You mean people actually talk like that?" That's the problem with our culture captured in a simple question: There's a pervasive sense that we don't *need* to learn to communicate about such body-emotion interplay, and so we don't.

Emotionally-Focused Therapy (EFT), which is what Trevor practices, has its roots in attachment theory, introduced in chapter 1. Susan Johnson's seminal work in EFT and the work of Diana Fosha in the mid-1990s make the connection between attachment theory, which we had considered only in terms of child development, and adult relationships. That connection is a breakthrough for relationship counseling.

Before turning to Trevor's venture into EFT, we want to spotlight a key connection between attachment styles and physical and mental health. If we have a secure attachment style, or through therapy and other relationships develop a secure attachment style, we are (among other things) better equipped to cope with stressful life events. Stress and illness feed on each other. It is a fact that stress substantially raises the risk of heart disease, cold, flu and much more.[8] The discussion of the biochemistry of this interplay is in chapter 3.

While studying marriage and family therapy, Trevor saw a video of Susan Johnson using EFT with a couple. Something happened in the session that she couldn't quite figure out. What Johnson was doing with the couple did not resemble anything therapists were learning or encouraged to do on the East Coast, although by then EFT had started to take root on the West Coast. At the time, Trevor was on the board of the Ackerman Institute for the Family in New York City. Founded in 1960 by Nathan Ackerman, it pioneered systemic therapy for families. At one of the board meetings, members heard that the Institute was joining forces with Susan Johnson to offer an externship. Trevor signed up immediately and became part of the first wave of therapists in the East to earn a certification in EFT. She had already done work with couples using the old-fashioned approach taught at the university: problem solving and having them practice the ten fair-fighting rules. The rules are things like "Don't call each other names" and "Don't use global words like 'always' and 'never' to describe the other person's behavior." This approach focuses on contents and, in a real way, turns a therapist into the umpire in the room. The therapist listens to the couple explain their problems and then offers an insight like, "She is right; you're wrong. Shape up!"

It is far from ideal. And many therapists who were doing it knew that it generally had no lasting effects. It's vital that the focus be on the interaction between people—the feelings that are being missed and the attunement that perhaps was never there. Trevor had had change moments with some couples, but didn't know why. Some came and went and she felt they never got any significant help.

In combining the work of Susan Johnson with that of Diana Fosha, who focuses more on physical processing than Johnson does, Trevor began to see some remarkable results with troubled couples. They woke up to the reality that, behind the behavior that related to difficulties in their relationship, there were attachment issues.

Your family of origin determines how you become attached or detached. You hadn't been seen or heard as a child; perhaps you hadn't been loved or valued. Those circumstances put stress on attachments and affect behavior in your relationships. You want something and aren't sure how to act to get it.

A spouse who feels he is not being valued by his marriage partner may well go out and find someone who will value him. A spouse who feels her partner does not pay attention to her needs may go to great lengths to call attention to those needs. Maybe she'll yell. Maybe she won't speak to him. Maybe she'll leave. A top-down approach to counseling in this situation might go like this: (to the man) "Next Sunday, instead of watching football, go for a walk with your wife." (to the woman) "The next time your husband wants to have sex, commit to it." A bottom-up approach is to delve into the attachment issues.

When you look at the landscape of a relationship problem through the lens of attachment theory, you see details and have a clear sense of how it evolved. Approaches learned in school don't have to be abandoned, but rather integrated differently.

Johnson was one of the first to explore how the push-pull between a partner who is "avoiding" and one who is "needy" affects both of them on the deepest level. The tension-filled relationship is not the secure attachment that both of them need, so their partnership is literally a sickening experience. Johnson summarizes what usually happens like this: "[A]ttachment theory…predicts that when attachment security is uncertain, a partner will pursue, fight, and even bully a spouse into responding to attachment cues, even if this has a negative general impact on the relationship."[9]

Because of attachment, we respond in a deeply emotional way when something goes wrong in our most intense relationships. We get over-reactive when we feel those relationships are under attack. The threat could be an argument with your partner or the sense you're being criticized or an incidence of infidelity. Regardless of what provoked it, your body has a fear response so you become over-reactive and less able to think. All of this is normal; it's part of a survival mechanism. It also takes a great toll on you.

In EFT therapy, clients sometimes shock the therapist with their sudden ability to express emotions. It's as though they had stored the raw ingredients of communication for a long time and a single incident seems to make them coalesce. Within the context of the emotionally-focused therapeutic environment, they learn to feel safe and, sometimes, they "let go."

Jen and Dean, a married couple, had been in counseling for four years. She was an angry, critical pursuer; he was a consistent avoider. In all that time, he had not articulated his feelings and seemed to avoid taking steps toward learning how. One day, Dean expressed his thoughts and emotions in a coherent and almost poetic way. He shook as though something possessing him was trying to escape his body. Jen was mesmerized. She asked him where this version of him had been all these years?

The triggering incident for this was Jen's discovery that he had tried to reconnect with his abusive mother. Dean felt he had never made an effort to help her face her demons and it haunted him. Instead of reacting with anger, which is what Trevor expected from Jen, she responded with forgiveness. Her outpouring of understanding—"This isn't about you trying to go behind my back, this is about you not forgiving yourself for incidents that happened years ago"—took him by surprise. It was as though her abrupt attitude change from her usual angry and critical stance immediately helped create a safe environment for him to express his feelings.

We're talking about a human relationship, so everything did not improve immediately. The backstory explains both the provocative reason that gave them the impetus to rebuild their connection as well as the mess they had to get through to have what we would call a "healthy connection."

They had a daughter who had been triangulated into their marriage in a diseased way. To some extent, Dean relied on her to give him the conversation and reassurance that should have been coming from his wife. The breakthrough her parents experienced set the stage for her easing out of that role and into her own life.

But there was still Jen's anger and the complexity of her feeling the blame for the failures in their marriage and with their children. It had driven her to have a sexual encounter with someone from the office, so she needed his forgiveness, too.

Let's add to that the residual effects—the biologically altering effects—of their traumatic childhoods. Divorce, alcoholism, parents' capricious behavior and other factors leading to emotional abandonment and inconsistency cluttered their backgrounds. Anxious attachment (angry pursuit) or persistent avoidance are how people normally respond to these circumstances.

Jen had pulled off a classic manipulation without even knowing it: using her focused anxiety and anger to get people to do what she wanted them to do at the law firm where she was a partner. Her competence was unmistakable but she seemed to emanate power because no one wanted to see her angry. Take that formula home and it's a recipe for disaster.

As a child, Dean had succeeded by always obeying his parents without objecting or voicing his point of view and excelling in school. His role as the good guy and caretaker positioned him in his family, and later his company, as someone others could count on to bring the team together and make things happen. And he did it all without getting emotionally involved. He brought that avoidance to his marriage just as Jen brought her anxiety.

After reading this description of Jen and Dean's dysfunctional relationship, you may be asking yourself why they would even want to stay together and why they had any hope that counseling could help them. Here's the provocative reason: Even in the worst of times, they couldn't keep their hands off one another. They had a magnetic, incredible sexual bond; splitting up represented a trauma that seemed far worse than a stressed-filled marriage.

Their satisfying sexual relationship represented an ongoing, co-regulating connection. Despite the anger she displayed on a daily basis, Dean referred to Jen in one of our sessions as his "sanctuary." A strong sexual bond does not always mean that two people often at odds can find peace with each other, so we wouldn't call their situation common.

Jen and Dean are still together. However their relationship has changed. Whereas she had been the pursuer in the relationship, demanding attention and angrily seeking it, he became the pursuer. For the avoidant (dismissive) Dean, the emotional floodgates opened—a phenomenon that can occur when there is a sudden realization of attachment security.[10]

The story of Jen and Dean illustrates that our brains are plastic; we can re-groove. The hope of a therapy like EFT is that we can go straight to the processes that enable us to re-groove.

We want to draw a further contrast between therapy that puts emotions at the center of issues and answers and therapy that puts a cognitive process at the center. The latter approach is far more well-known and popular in this culture, but it is inconsistent with the fundamental message of this book. Probably the most popular is Cognitive-Behavioral Therapy (CBT). CBT is prominent in our American culture because we pride ourselves on being able to think through problems and use what we consider our superior intellects to handle every troubling issue that comes along.

"Deciding" and "thinking" alone don't make people change. If you tell a cigarette smoker, "Stop smoking. Just make a decision and do it," that will not work. People don't make a big change unless they are emotionally invested in it. You can decide to stop smoking, but the thread running through the decision and the result is emotion. Try telling a toddler to stop screaming in the middle of a tantrum; it doesn't work. A smoker is as emotionally invested in smoking as the toddler is in throwing the tantrum. Neither can cognitively turn off their behavior.

The National Association of Cognitive-Behavior Therapists defines CBT on their website:

> *Cognitive-Behavioral Therapy is a form of psychotherapy that emphasizes the important role of thinking in how we feel and what we do.*
>
> *...**CBT is based on the Cognitive Model of Emotional Response.** Cognitive-behavioral therapy is based on the idea that our thoughts cause our feelings and behaviors, not external things, like people, situations, and events. The benefit of this fact is that we can change the way we think to feel/act better even if the situation does not change.*[11]

We have ample evidence in neurological and psychiatric research that thinking in the absence of emotional input is ineffective. In *Descartes' Error*, Antonio Damasio illustrates this point in the example of Phineas Gage.[12] A railroad construction accident damaged Gage's brain, leaving him without his ability to generate emotions. He was physically incapable of making moral and socially acceptable decisions. He became a total reprobate when the injury he suffered essentially severed the connections between the emotional and cognitive portions of his brain. Damasio asserts this makes René Descartes ("I think, therefore I am."[13]) wrong in arguing the idea that the human mind is separate from bodily processes. We join Damasio in re-scripting the defining element of humanity, "You feel, therefore you are."

There is a widespread acceptance in our culture—reinforced by numerous self-help books—that thinking through problems, deciding to change, positive thinking and so on, yield measurable results. Translation: Therapy like CBT that is thought-based is reimbursable by insurance companies. Even though the patient's change may be short term, the change occurred and is documented, making therapy like CBT "evidence-based."

Change actually involves emotion, however. The bridge between deciding to do something and getting a result (for example, changing a behavior) is emotion. The right brain jumps in and infuses the decision with some kind of emotional significance.[14] What therapists using talk therapy such as EFT work with is the strength and authenticity of that emotion. In essence, the power of the emotion correlates to the endurance of the change.

The underlying body chemistry of this change is the shift to a de-stressed state that the emotionally-focused work elicits. When the therapeutic experience engenders co-regulation, our bodies increase production of hormones related to positive feelings, communication and trust. Thinking about putting ourselves in a positive, change-committed space is not the same as doing it; feeling is *doing* it as evidenced by the changes in our body.

A defining moment in Trevor's career as a therapist came early. It was the first time she realized that her education hadn't taught her what she needed to know to help people in times of trouble. She had not yet absorbed the wisdom of "You feel, therefore you are."

She started her career as a therapist at Fairfield Community Counseling, which invited anyone to get the benefits of services regardless of what they could afford to pay. Three women came in for help: a young woman with multiple learning challenges, her mother and her aunt. They lived together in poverty and had lots of interpersonal struggles. After trying to find out about the positive aspects of their relationship, they started talking about braiding each other's hair. Trevor did not get it, but listened nonetheless to figure out why this was important.

When times were hardest, this is something they did to feel better. In reality, their way of showing each other love was the grooming ritual of braiding each other's hair. That action shows how the physical aspect of our relationships can be so inextricably linked to deep emotion and healthy attachments.

Braiding each other's hair cost no money, brought them into close contact with each other, gave them time to talk and made them all feel more attractive at the end. We all need some version of braiding each other's hair.

Would a CBT therapist have helped them by proceeding on the premise that our "thoughts cause our feelings and behaviors"? These women taught Trevor the lesson that health and healing have their roots in emotions.

"FULL-BODIED" MEANS MULTI-GENERATIONAL

Our bodies contain and express what has happened to us in terms of safe haven—not just in our own lifetimes, but also in our parents' and grandparents' lifetimes. Disorders induced by trauma can have multi-generational effects. But if there is a "yin," there is a "yang." The good stuff induced by happiness and prosperity can have multi-generational effects, too, as indicated by a number of studies.

Before exploring the science of how this happens, we want to point out that the research in this field is recent, having occurred in the latter part of the twentieth and early part of the twenty-first centuries. In the 1980s, Swedish researchers tracked the long-term effects of famine and found that an environmental trauma of that magnitude could be experienced for multiple generations. They determined that it actually left a genetic imprint. This left Charles Darwin's theory of evolution looking a bit dusty, because it meant that new health problems could take shape and be passed on in a single generation.[15]

After the Human Genome Project released results of its work in 2000, efforts continued to completely understand the genetic makeup of human beings.[16] The Human Genome Project is an international research project to determine the sequence of chemical base pairs which make up DNA, and of identifying and mapping the 20,000–25,000 genes in the complete set of human genetic information from both a physical and functional standpoint. A great many quasi-scientific stories floated around trying to explain obesity, alcoholism, autism and so on with the platitude, "He has the gene for (fill in the blank with the name of a health problem)." Having a gene is only part of the equation. The gene also has to express itself and genes need help to do that. They can be activated or deactivated. To phrase that more proactively, the process of turning some genes on and turning others off is normal and necessary, but our responses to environmental stimuli can also effect that activation or deactivation.

Both occur in the womb.

Genes responsible for the development of the lens in the eye need to be shut down at some point or the lens would be so thick we couldn't see through it. Those same genes need to be activated at the proper time for the lens to develop. There is another wondrous aspect of this process: All of the cells in our body contain the same genes, but some may be expressed depending on where they are located, for example, in the lungs versus the brain.

In addition to these normal changes in expression, the pregnant mother's response to environmental stimuli can also trigger activation or deactivation of gene expression. This becomes an inheritable trait when the fetus is female because her body contains eggs—and those eggs represent the pregnant woman's grandchildren!

Studies that were highly complementary to the one done by the Swedish team began to focus on inherited changes in gene expression, not just whether or not a particular gene could be seen in an individual's genomic map. Studies involving rats showed a direct correlation between variations in the way the mother cared for her pups and the effect it had over generations on behavioral responses as well as endocrine responses, that is, those related to secretion of hormones into the bloodstream. A team at McGill University in Montreal, Canada, found that mothers who licked and coddled their pups reinforced their ability to react to stress, essentially boosting their immune systems; the opposite effect was associated with the less attentive moms. Not only was that causal relationship between maternal behavior and pup health demonstrated, but the researchers also saw that there was a transmission of the tendencies to the subsequent generation. The conclusion was this: "Taken together, these findings indicate that variations in maternal care can serve as the basis for nongenomic behavioral transmission of individual differences in stress reactivity across generations."[17]

It's the same with human mothers. Studies of how stress affects mother-child interaction have indicated that moms experiencing stressful lives, or at least episodes of stress, were less sensitive and more punitive than unstressed mothers. The quality of care they gave suffered seriously. The physical impact that the researchers documented is that the stressed mother had a disruption to her autonomic (think "automatic") nervous system, which reflected the fact that the right hemisphere of her brain was affected by the stress. With the autonomic nervous system responsible for controlling the organs, certain skin responses and the cardiovascular system, it's easy to see how stress potentially affected the health and well-being of both mother and baby. When that baby becomes an adult, her responses to stress will reveal what she went through early in life, and her children may also feel the effects.

Research supporting that assertion of multi-generational impact is compelling. A study conducted by the University of British Columbia's Centre for Molecular Medicine and Therapeutics in 2012 pinpointed the correlations between immune responses and stress-causing factors like childhood poverty and distressed adult relationships. The year before, the lead on that study, Michael Kobor, published the results of related research documenting how parents' stress leaves a negative imprint on the DNA of their children.[18]

The reason that the change may not stop with those directly affected by the stress is that a process affecting genetic expression can take place; that may result in an inherited change.

One process in charge is called DNA methylation, which Kobor describes as a kind of dimmer switch on gene function.[19] DNA methylation means adding a methyl group to a particular region of the DNA; the methyl group makes it difficult for the gene to be expressed. Methylation plays a crucial role in the development of an organism, and it is a main factor in the normal activation and deactivation process that we described previously. So, it not only impacts gene expression, but it also affects cellular differentiation in human beings. (That's kind of like giving your cells job descriptions.) It's important to note that DNA methylation affects only the expression of genes—not the genes themselves. It's responsible for enabling cells to "remember where they have been" to repeat patterns or for decreasing the expression of genes.[20]

Trauma can have an effect on DNA methylation that's potentially devastating to a person's health. Whether it's a personal trauma like having a very stressed-out mother or a community-wide trauma like the Holocaust, the specific type of change in DNA methylation that it can trigger is a long-term dysregulation of the stress hormone system. In other words, trauma may render the victims less able to cope with stressful situations.[21] They may develop depression, anxiety disorders, post-traumatic stress disorder or other so-called "mental problems." But as we know, people who suffer from these issues are also more vulnerable to other types of disease. For example, depressed people tend to be low-energy and don't have the "fight" to fend off illnesses—from the common cold to cancer.

The evidence of the changes caused by methylation is not just subjective; it is the result of researchers studying a population and recording rises in certain illnesses that seem to correlate with traumatic events. Some researchers have combined those records with actual measurements of how methylated the genes of victims are. One such study involved multiple generations affected by the Dutch famine known as the *Hongerwinter* or Hunger Winter. In the winter of 1944-1945, German soldiers cut off food shipments from the farming region to densely populated areas of the Netherlands. An estimated 4.5 million people were affected. The researchers focused on the offspring of women who were pregnant that winter, taking blood samples from them to measure the methylation state of certain genes. These people were over sixty years old at the time of the study and they did show an increased level of methylation as compared to their siblings who were born just before or just after the Hunger Winter.[22] Neurobiologist Paul Patterson articulates a widely held conclusion in his book *Infectious Behavior*:

*"The results of the Dutch Hunger Winter study, coupled
with animal studies, indicate that epigenetic changes in the
fetus that were driven by the maternal environment can
be permanent. There is also evidence that some epigenetic
changes are heritable across generations."*[23]

At the beginning of this section, we suggested that there is a
"yang" counterpart to the "yin." Dawson Church, a health writer and
researcher, coined the term "epigenetic medicine" to describe the opposite of what we've been describing. That is, instead of focusing on
the inheritable negative outcomes, he builds epigenetic arguments for
positive outcomes triggered by beliefs and emotions.[24] Similarly, James
Baird, Laurie Nadel and Bruce H. Lipton—researchers with PhDs in
natural health, psychology and developmental biology, respectively—
argue in their book *Happiness Genes* that genetic expression can be
impacted by beliefs and emotions.[25]

What is clearly needed on the "plus" side of the genetic expression equation is more research from a broad community of professionals in research science as well as clinical practice. Immunologist
Kim Burnham of Oklahoma State University is doing measurements
of the impact of social factors on cellular and molecular components
of the immune system; work such as his may yield further clues about
multi-generational effects.[26]

A summary of the emerging gene science appeared in *Psychology
Today* in 2011. Award-winning journalist Ariel Gore ended her article,
"Epigenetics, Save Me From My Family!" by referencing Church's book
Genie in Your Genes, which cites studies showing the value of positive
and de-stressing interaction on DNA expression "within seconds."[27]
Gore states:

"This insta-healing might still be a stretch for conventional scientists, but it's now common knowledge that

1) We have more control over our DNA than we've been led to
   believe, and

2) While we can't change the sequence of our DNA, we may be able to change whether or not it's activated."[28]

From a clinical perspective, there is a great body of evidence to support the argument for the positive, multi-generational effects of strong tribal and intimate connections. A common example among humans where we often see the "good news" carried forward is adoption. If you adopt a child at birth, by the time the child is roughly twenty-one, he is—in part, in reality—your biological child. The influence you have on the child is so profound that it changes the structure and function of the brain, including what that adopted child passes on to his children. Such a change could occur because the relationship you have impacts a key genetic process.

To understand this better, let's return to the rat pups studies done by the Montreal team. It's relatively straightforward to observe that offspring of negligent mothers carried that forward to their own parenting and that they had heightened stress responses. It was also evident that the effect carried on to the subsequent generation. How can we be sure the explanation doesn't lie in the genes, rather than the expression of them?

The researchers essentially put the pups up for adoption. Pups of stressed out, negligent mothers went to the superior caregivers and vice versa. The traits they exhibited reflected the environmental influence of the adoptive mother, not the biological one. Those traits were then passed on to the next generation.[29]

The interplay of genetic and environmental factors not only affects the expression of our genes, but that expression can also be passed on to future descendants. A disproportionately high number of individuals in a population with a significant shared experience— war, for example—might manifest certain traits and pass them on simply because the experience of war affected all of them similarly on a genetic level.

The effects don't stop with the individual person affected by the DNA methylation change. The change itself is an inheritable trait.

The permanent epigenetic marks left by trauma on a single person or many of the individuals in a community can surface in the next generation and the next one after that.

A single event can therefore have health effects on a population for decades.

There is no scientific reason to dilute or equivocate on the main point we're making: Both nature and nurture play significant roles in the health and well-being of individuals and their offspring—and *their* offspring. As partners, caregivers, parents and other contributors to society, each of us has an ability to affect the present and future states of the health of our families and tribes.

CHAPTER 3

Fear Up, Fear Down

A sense of security is not a feeling or state to be avoided. Rather, it's a healthful way to live and the natural and desired outcome of strong connections with other human beings. The positive, physical effects of a secure relationship do powerful and practical things for our bodies and our sense of risk-taking and competence.

In biochemical terms, when we are relaxed and feeling safe our bodies make more feel-good hormones, like oxytocin and opiates. We are predisposed to be healthier. When we're stressed, under some kind of physical or psychological threat, we make hormones that wear down our immune system.

FEAR UP: WHAT HAPPENS TO YOU?

Fear is a powerful negative emotion that takes shape out of the belief that someone or something is dangerous, either physically or psychologically. For many people, having to speak in public evokes a fear response; a first date could do the same. Even though you might call those situations "challenges" rather than fear-inducing events, for some people they provoke a response in the autonomic (automatic) nervous system that's extreme. As far as their bodies are concerned, they might as well be in a dark alley facing an armed assailant.

In an intense relationship, your partner has the ability to put you into a fear state very quickly. The behavior could be anger, criticism, betrayal or withdrawal, for example, but you feel attacked because your sense of self and your trust in the relationship are threatened.

There are two models we use to describe what happens to you when you are in a fear-up state. The first is a classic explanation involving the sympathetic and parasympathetic nervous system. The second is a very new model called The Polyvagal Theory.

SYMPATHETIC-PARASYMPATHETIC MODEL

Walter Cannon did pioneering work in fear responses, coining the phrase "fight or flight" in 1929. Cannon was chairman of the department of Physiology at Harvard Medical School in the early twentieth century and was known for pinpointing how our fear responses are unavoidable, that is, we can't think them away.[1] Since then, ethologists (scientists who study animal behavior) have helped us fine-tune the understanding of what happens to the body in the face of a threat.

Jeffrey A. Gray added a third element to Cannon's description: the freeze response.[2] This is a normal survival response in which the person goes into a hyper-vigilant state immediately after sensing a threat. Watch animals go into this state as a predator that moves much faster than they do approaches. It's an attempt to avoid detection by remaining perfectly still, otherwise known as "playing dead." That is a freeze response in which the animal's muscles are loose. There is another type in which the body is on high alert and muscles are taut. As part of this freeze response, pupils dilate to take in more information about the situation. (Related to connection, our pupils dilate when we're attracted to someone, too. Again, our bodies want to take in as much information as possible!)[3]

According to Gray, the next response would be the attempt to flee, so there's an assertion that Cannon's sequence was backwards and should be revised to "flight or fight." That's not necessarily the case, however, even though it may apply to most people. The reason for this is that we can be trained, such as in the military or certain sports, to override the flight response and go straight into attack mode. Put this style of reacting into the context of a business or personal situation and you have people instantly going on the offensive when someone "threatens" them with "You don't know what you're talking about!" or "I don't believe you!"

Regardless of what comes next, fight or flight, when we are under attack, either in a physical or psychological sense, the body goes into overdrive. As a person's stress level rises, the adrenal gland—also known as the "stress gland"—gets active. First, it generates adrenaline, and then the cortisol cycle kicks in. Within milliseconds of the initial threat that triggered the cortisol cycle, the sympathetic nervous system revs up. The sympathetic is the part of our peripheral nervous system that agitates the body; its counterpart, the parasympathetic system, handles rest and relaxation responses. And then, in addition to fueling us with cortisol and adrenaline, the adrenal gland also produces DHEA (dehydroepiandrosterone), which is the most abundant steroid circulating in the human body.[4]

Everything that the stress hormones are going to do to your body to prepare it for fight or flight happens almost instantaneously. The body, not the mind, decides which systems are needed for the perceived threat. These systems turn on at the cost of others that the body does not consider necessary at the moment.

Fight or Flight: Inside
- Blood leaves the face and skin, goes to the muscles.
- Blood goes away from digestive, reproductive systems.
- Can't contract the bladder and expel waste.
- Glucose heads to liver to prepare for physical activity.
- Blood flows to reptilian (survival) and mammalian (emotion) brains at the expense of the primate (cognitive) brain.

- Heart action escalates to get blood to the right places.
- Respiration increases to fuel muscles with oxygen.
- Metabolism heightens, so the body starts to sweat.
- Pupils dilate to collect data about the threat.[5]

Fight or Flight: Outside
> Note: *Some signs will occur only in situations where the person perceives an extreme threat to safety.*

- Pallid complexion
- Drooping lower eyelids
- Pounding of chest
- Hands may shake
- Flared nostrils and audible breathing
- Eyes focused on the cause of stress—squinting or wide open
- Brow clinches and draws downward
- Lips tighten to a thin, colorless line
- Shoulders draw higher in preparation for defense or escape
- White residue in corners of the mouth
- Elbows close to the ribs
- Palms turn down and the hands close to form fists
- Fight or flight body odor
- Ultimately, collapse[6]

Once you've experienced the fear that triggers a fight-or-flight response, the mere memory of it can do the same thing. A region in the brain called the amygdala has a key role in processing memory and emotional reactions. It makes a connection between the original experience and a stimulus that reminds you of the fear-inducing incident. Maybe you were petting the neighbor's new dog one day and it bit you. It's possible that just seeing a dog that looks like it will activate the amygdala and you will feel the same fear as you did when the dog bit you. It's an automatic response, just as your physical fight-or-flight reactions to the original danger were an automatic response.

THE POLYVAGAL THEORY

Stephen W. Porges, PhD, professor of Psychiatry and Bioengineering and director of the Brain-Body Center at the University of Illinois at Chicago, doesn't see the paired antagonism model of sympathetic-parasympathetic as a complete explanation of fear-up/fear-down in the body.

The Polyvagal Theory reflects his work on the autonomic nervous system and it has led to a fresh perspective on what happens to the body when a threat is present. As part of that theory, Porges also has a unique take on how social interactions help regulate the body, and he makes a direct link between fight-flight and its impact on well-being and the restoration of health.

"Poly" means many; "vagal" refers to the vagus nerve, which has the important job of carrying information about the body to the brain. The word "polyvagal" captures the fact that activity of the vagus can occur in different areas of the brain—that is, there are multiple vagal pathways—at the same time it's telling the brain what's happening in your heart, lungs and other organs.

In the section just cited on the sympathetic-parasympathetic model, we mentioned that fear responses and many of the balancing responses that relate to calm are automatic, meaning that they reflect activity of the autonomic nervous system. We don't control it; it just does its job of making sure we are breathing, have a heartbeat and are digesting food, among other things. The vagus plays a part in the autonomic nervous system because it's the primary conduit for the parasympathetic nervous system. Most of the body activity related to making you feel safe and relaxed comes through the vagus.

To express why the Polyvagal Theory is so important here, we will over-simplify Porges' scientific explanation: The theory involves a three-tiered hierarchy when it comes to a state of fear-up/fear-down. We call them old vagus, sympathetic system and new vagus, but you can also think of them in terms of what they do:

Old vagus – shuts you down
Sympathetic system – gets you going
New vagus – makes you social

"Old vagus" is the part of the nerve that's reptilian. If you have ever seen a mouse play dead when a cat catches it, you have seen the old vagus in action. It shuts down heartbeat and breathing; the animal goes completely limp and the predator figures it's already dead so it's less interesting. That's fine for reptiles, which do not require a lot of oxygen to survive. Unfortunately for the mouse, or any other oxygen-hungry mammal, that autonomic response can have fatal consequences. Many mice die in the jaws of the cat, not because the cat clamped down on them with its incisors, but because of the old vagus trying to do its job. In the list of internal responses to fight or flight, we noted the impact of fear on the digestive system. This shutting down of digestive function is an example of the old vagus affecting the human body.

As we said in the last section, the sympathetic nervous system involves adrenaline and cortisol shooting into your body to mobilize you. The freeze response that you might have—not playing dead, but a state of stillness, muscle tautness and high alertness—is actually a sympathetic response rather than one related to the old vagus.

"New vagus" relates to calming down your heart rate and your breathing and putting you in a state where you can interact socially. It sits on top of the sympathetic nervous system in the hierarchy. With that in mind, let's reverse the order in the stack to show what has the most influence on you and what has the least in this model:

New vagus – makes you social
Sympathetic system – gets you going
Old vagus – shuts you down

Porges refers to the "vagal brake" in explaining how the new vagus operates and, specifically, how it relates to making us social.[7] We want the brake on when we are in safe situations with people we trust. We can be energetic and dynamic without stimulating the sympathetic nervous system. So with our vagal brake on, we have the ability to be active without turning on the powerful engine that serves us in fight or flight. When the brake is released, we unleash the sympathetic responses.

This is the big difference between the classic antagonistic model and Porges' model: Instead of having two systems in play to explain how our body responds to different situations and people, he added a third, and that third one links directly to how we behave as social beings.

This hierarchy is only one part of the two main parts of the Polyvagal Theory, however. The other is the face-heart connection. On one level, this part is intuitive. On another, it sheds light on the science behind how we make connections with other people and, ultimately, the role those connections play in staying healthy as well as the restoration of health.

The science behind this is that the nerves of the face and the nerves that regulate our heart and lungs are linked. The nerves that trigger a response in the face and head all connect in the brain stem to the area that controls the "new vagus." Whether the vagal brake is on or off, our face will show it.

That means the face reveals what's going on for us viscerally, sometimes with a great deal of precision. Studies conducted by Dr. Paul Ekman confirmed that human beings have certain facial expressions in common: disgust, sadness, anger, fear, surprise and happiness. But there is an entire range of facial expressions beyond these that we can often read, particularly if we know the person. The problem is that we are sometimes so cognitive, listening to the words someone is saying and perhaps thinking through what we're going to say, that we completely miss the emotion being expressed. From an evolutionary standpoint, these facial expressions are supposed to give us a clue as to whether or not the person is safe to be with: Is the person a threat, or someone who makes us feel safe? Or to use Porges' term again, is the brake on or off?

The Polyvagal Theory isn't just a way of explaining what happens in the body in fear-up or fear-down conditions. Porges sees it as a tool to help clinicians develop new ways of helping people with physical and mental illnesses. He says if we're in a state of fight or flight, our ability to be social is compromised. This affects the ability of a doctor to treat a patient. A physician needs to recruit neural circuits that not only support social behavior, but also support health and well-being. The same circuits that are involved in social behavior are also involved in health, growth and restoration.[8]

FEAR UP: WHY IT MAKES YOU SICK

What's so bad about having a hyperactive sympathetic nervous system? It may seem counterintuitive that a nervous system so necessary for our survival would jeopardize our survival. The underlying logic is that we actually have more than one type of immune system, with the release of hormones during fight or flight having a positive effect on one and a negative effect on the other.

The two types of immune systems are innate and adaptive (or humeral). The first responds quickly to infection or injury; it's the innate system that benefits from the sympathetic nervous system going into high gear. The second responds more slowly to environmental challenges. The adaptive "figures out" what kind of antibodies are needed to counter an invasion of disease and then begins to produce them. In the face of stress—even a mild fear-up situation—the body diverts resources away from the adaptive immune system and directs them into the innate immune system.

So even though we need cortisol to live, it wreaks havoc with our adaptive immune system. Here is the basic scenario: The cortisol surge as part of a fight-or-flight response breaks down tissues and increases the level of blood sugar. In addition, cortisol decreases bone formation. DHEA theoretically comes to the rescue by bolstering the immune system and repairing tissues. We say "theoretically" because DHEA levels begin to drop after we turn thirty, and they can also be affected negatively by a number of health conditions and drugs, like insulin and corticosteroids. So even though the human body is fundamentally made to rebound from fear episodes, that recovery may not happen and thus health is jeopardized.

As we discussed in the beginning of this chapter, a sense of security is not something to avoid, but rather something to seek. The opposite—a state of fight or flight—is to be avoided for your psychological and physical health because, when it recurs because of your life situation, your immune system takes round after round of beating and, at some point, it's "knocked out." A deficient immune system makes you vulnerable to infections of all kinds; you don't have the ability to fend off invaders.

The link between chronic stress and a weakened immune system has an interesting dimension that seems to involve the sympathetic nervous system expanding. Steve W. Cole, a professor at the UCLA School of Medicine whose area of research is psycho-neuro-immunology, found that young monkeys put under chronic stress had double the number of sympathetic nerves in their lymph nodes after a few months. The phenomenon did not occur everywhere in the lymph nodes, just in certain regions. The health-related consequences could be rather dramatic since the growth in the lymph nodes can have a major effect on how a body responds to infection.[9]

In his book, *Infectious Behavior*, neurobiologist Paul H. Patterson draws in Cole's work as part of an elegant way of expressing the pathway from chronic stress to disease progression. Chronic stress suppresses production of proteins called interferons, which cells release when the body is being attacked by a virus, bacteria or other pathogens. Their job is enabling communication among cells that serves as a kind of call-to-arms to the immune system. So with the reduced production of interferon, the pathway Patterson describes is:

Chronic social stress → enhanced growth of sympathetic nerves in the lymph node → reduction of interferon production → increased viral replication → disease progression during social stress.[10]

Unfortunately, there's more bad news when it comes to chronic psychological stress and damage to the immune system. In a biological version of "if it's not one thing, it's another!" an additional pathway from stress to sickness starts with the cerebral cortex, which recognizes something as a source of stress. That perception gets communicated to the hypothalamus, the portion of the brain that is responsible for regulating certain autonomic functions such as digestion and heart rate. The hypothalamus sends a red alert to the pituitary gland, which is an endocrine gland at the base of the hypothalamus. Endocrine glands secrete hormones; in this case some of the hormones from the pituitary gland influence immune cells. The pituitary passes them on to the adrenal gland, which is also an endocrine gland. It also secretes hormones, most importantly cortisol and adrenaline, both of which affect immune cells as we noted above. The pathway that we just described has a fairly straightforward name: the hypothalamic-pituitary-adrenal (HPA) axis.[11]

Integral to the process that damages the immune system is the development of a faulty feedback loop because of the outpouring of cortisol. Too much of it circulating in the body can have toxic effects on the part of the brain responsible for memory, the hippocampus. The body wants to take care of itself, so when it detects too much cortisol, it takes action with cortisol receptors. And so, the hippocampus simply becomes less responsive to cortisol. The hippocampus then takes a dive in its effectiveness. Consider this explanation when someone with a lot of stress in her life tells you she's having trouble remembering things.

Patterson makes a couple of unequivocal statements about the cause and effect relationships of stress and illness:

> *"...even mild, acute stress affects the immune system. Lymphocytes [white blood cells in the immune system] taken from healthy subjects who underwent a mildly stressful experience, such as speaking in front of a group of volunteers, exhibit elevated markers of inflammation. It is notable that such responses to acute stress are exaggerated in patients with major depressive disorder.*

*...Results from animal studies indicate that the sup-
pression of the immune response that occurs with chronic
stress can indeed increase vulnerability to infections and
disease. Moreover, in humans, there is evidence that both
major depressive disorder and chronic stress are associated
with increased susceptibility to a variety of problems such
as respiratory infection, cardiovascular disease, and HIV/
AIDS. Each of these conditions is known to involve systemic inflammation."* [12]

A related piece of the puzzle comes from multiple teams of researchers who have concluded that emotional, psychological and environmental stress influence brain function. Specifically, stress causes
a breakdown in the blood-brain barrier (BBB), which separates blood
circulating your body from the brain fluid in your central nervous
system. It prevents certain types of large molecules, such as bacteria,
from flowing into the brain fluid, but allows others, such as hormones,
to get through. The laboratory studies about the relationship between
stress and brain dysfunction have been going on for decades but it
wasn't until a key paper on the subject came out in 2010 that researchers concluded, "it appears that the BBB is the *gateway* to neuropsychi-
atric diseases." [13] Then they went on to discuss the altered cognitive and
sensory-motor functions related to stress-induced brain dysfunction.

In working with couples and families struggling through issues
that turn the heat up on the stress in their lives, Trevor often sees
something quite encouraging: On some level, they actually realize
they're making themselves and each other sick. They seem to enjoy—
and need—coming into a safe environment where they can let their
antagonism seep through the floorboards.

Any of us who have ever experienced chronic stress—and who
hasn't?—can appreciate the alternative and what it represents: the
ability to heal.

Dr. Judith Orloff, assistant clinical professor of Psychiatry at
UCLA, tells the story of her mother, a family medical practitioner. At

age seventy, Orloff's mother decided to take her national board exam, a grueling test that she committed to taking so she could keep up with the younger doctors. She had a thriving practice and many patients who loved her, including the Rolling Stones' Mick Jagger. "A million people who look at her and tell her how wonderful she was and she would only look at her negative points, her self-doubts."[14]

Twenty years prior to facing that exam, Orloff's mother had been diagnosed with a benign lymphoma. While she was studying for the test—all the while criticizing herself for not being good enough—the cell type changed to a malignant leukemia. Orloff's mother passed the test and shortly thereafter, she died. As she was dying, Orloff's mother told her daughter that she believed the stress of the test caused the cell type to change.[15]

Orloff has carried the lessons of her mother's life and death forward in her bestselling books and her workshops on transforming negative emotions and achieving inner peace.

FEAR DOWN: HOW CAN YOU MAKE IT HAPPEN?

Since the onset of fight-or-flight responses happens automatically, it's very helpful to know what will trigger them so that you can structure your life, as much as possible, to avert them. That is, what makes you afraid?

Maryann was doing a lecture on understanding body language at George Mason University and introduced the topic of fear with a photo of an American badger that she took in her front yard. In case you've never seen a badger, it's a small, vicious predator with claws so large and sharp that the animal can dig through rocky ground and create a tunnel opening in minutes. It will attack at the slightest provocation. (Badgers didn't learn the protocol to flee first.) One woman in Maryann's audience who had previously encountered a badger gasped audibly when she saw the photo. Her breathing became rapid, her eyes grew large and she put her hand over her heart. A simple photograph had triggered a fight-or-flight response. Her experience points out two things: Different people have different thresholds for experiencing fear and different people have different reference points regarding fear.

Let's distinguish between anxiety and fear even though the response of our bodies may initially be the same. A standard differentiation, captured in a January 2012 *New York Times* article, is:

> *"Scientists generally define fear as a negative emotional state triggered by the presence of a stimulus that has the potential to cause harm, and anxiety as a negative emotional state in which the threat is not present but anticipated."*[16]

However, it doesn't necessarily make a difference to your sympathetic nervous system if you feel terrorized by the signal or symbol of something threatening—the sound of a police siren behind you on the highway—or the actual threat appears in front of you in the form of a derisive sheriff writing you a ticket. Ivan Pavlov showed this with his conditioning experiments with dogs, which came to associate a bell ringing with meal time; they salivated at the sound of the bell whether or not their dinner ever arrived. Anticipation of an outcome, especially a threat, can therefore have powerful physical repercussions.

After the massacre of children and teachers at Sandy Hook Elementary School, we thought about this level of anxiety in relation to the proposal made by the head of the National Rifle Association. He urged the nation to post armed guards at schools to avert similar incidents.[17] Children across the nation, not just the survivors of Sandy Hook, had just been traumatized by the thought of a person with a gun at school. The idea of making children see an armed person at their school *every day* would not signal security for some or perhaps even most of them. That armed person could end up being nothing more than a stark reminder of the murders and a cause for repeatedly experiencing anxiety. What would that do to the children's immune systems?

The experience of fear is often associated with phobias, like fear of heights or fear of crowds. A major reason for the development of phobias is that we associate danger with the situation or thing—and have no control over them. Many people associate extreme panic with the idea of "jumping out of a perfectly good airplane;" they don't see a parachute as giving them control over a dangerous situation. But traumatic events can also cause a phobia to take hold. Being bullied as a child, for example, could trigger a social phobia. The person could develop such low self-esteem and feelings of inferiority that the connections—the type of connections we're talking about that support health and well-being—may seem out of reach.

Dr. John Biever, co-author with Maryann of *The Wandering Mind: Understanding Dissociation from Daydreams to Disorders*, once encountered a child whose greatest fear had been dormant for years. When the cause of that fear returned, his physical response to the perceived threat was both unusual and profound.[18]

While Dr. Biever was supervising psychiatry residents in a medication clinic for children at Penn State's Hershey Medical Center, a nine-year-old boy with Attention Deficit Disorder came in for his periodic medication check. He'd done well during the couple of years he had been taking medication for the problem but during this visit his grandmother requested a change. The boy had started complaining about a crawling sensation on his arms and her research indicated that the medication might be the culprit.[19]

John strongly disapproved of the standard fifteen-minute medication check—and we completely agree since it gives the clinician only about eight minutes of working time with the patient—so he had the doctors under his supervision allocate thirty minutes. That gave him the extra time he needed to talk to the grandmother rather than simply agree or disagree with her conclusion and write a new prescription.

He learned that the grandmother had been estranged from the boy's mother for several years. One afternoon, the grandmother and one of her friends saw a little boy dumpster-diving for food. Flies covered his arms. The grandmother was horrified; she was even more horrified when her friend told her, "That's your grandson." The grandmother had never met the child due to the broken relationship with her daughter. Immediately, she sought and received legal custody of the boy.[20]

John asked the grandmother about the boy's current circumstances. He learned that the boy's mother had recently, without warning, showed up at her home. The boy had not seen her since the day his grandmother rescued him from the dumpster. He immediately showed signs of extreme fear.

John speculated that maybe there was a correlation between the boy seeing his mother and her threatening to re-enter his life and getting the feeling that bugs were crawling on him. He was experiencing a traumatic memory. The grandmother reassured John and her grandson that she would never allow the mother to take him away. The boy soon regained a sense of safe haven with his grandmother and the crawling sensation went away.[21]

It isn't simply the disaster of fifteen-minute med checks that undermines the kind of therapeutic interaction that could help people like this little boy. In some types of therapy—those with roots in the past—emotion is still a bad word. The child's behavior would not be understood as indicative of something deeper. The role of fear in his symptoms might not have been explored.

When people experience phobias, they might as well be facing an armed assailant or a grizzly bear. Here are some of the symptoms:

- Feeling of panic, dread, horror or terror
- Recognition that the fear goes beyond normal boundaries and the actual threat of danger
- Reactions that are automatic and uncontrollable, practically taking over the person's thoughts
- Rapid heartbeat, shortness of breath, trembling and an overwhelming desire to flee the situation—all the physical reactions associated with extreme fear
- Extreme measures taken to avoid the feared object or situation[22]

Therapists who treat phobias may choose various treatment routes, depending on the patient, the phobia and their particular orientation as therapists. Of course, there are also non-therapists, such as motivational speaker Anthony Robbins, who helped launch their careers by successfully "treating" people with phobias. Their approach is some form of exposure therapy, that is, putting the phobic individual in direct contact with the source of his or her fear to prove that the anticipated, horrible consequences won't happen. A variation of this is a common part of team-building exercises that companies use to strengthen connections between co-workers. An example is the trust fall, which involves one person standing on a table or platform and falling backwards into the arms of co-workers. We think there are better ways than this to engender meaningful connections with people at the office.

Another route is systematic desensitization, pioneered by Joseph Wolpe, who felt that using drugs to treat patients with what we now call post-traumatic stress disorder fell far short in helping them recover. Wolpe did much of his best-known work while a professor of psychiatry at Temple University's Medical School from 1965 to 1988. He based his technique on the premise that neurotic disorders (and he looked at phobias as among them) are largely learned and, since they come from our experiences, having other experiences that run counter to them might be corrective.[23]

You can relate to the logic of this if, for example, your high school boyfriend broke your heart so you felt afraid of relationships for years. Then you met Mr. Right and the repeated good experiences with him conditioned you to no longer fear intimacy. In short, Wolpe's premise seems much more attuned to human nature and needs than a pharmaceutical "cure" for fears and anxiety. Desensitization involves three steps:

1. Train the patient to physically relax.
2. Establish an anxiety hierarchy of the stimuli involved.
3. Apply counter-conditioning relaxation as a response to each feared stimulus, beginning first with the least anxiety-provoking stimulus and moving then to the next least anxiety-provoking stimulus until all of the items listed in the anxiety hierarchy have been dealt with successfully.[24]

What Wolpe did, then, was take a methodical approach to getting the parasympathetic nervous system to kick in and rescue the individual so that the body calms down and fight-or-flight responses subside. The brain starts to function well again and those internal and external signs of a hyperactive sympathetic nervous system abate.

Let's look at some research which illustrates another way to arouse the parasympathetic system that involves the simple touch of a loved one.

University of Virginia psychologist Dr. James Coan's study, published in the journal *Psychological Science* in 2006, illustrates the effect of a positive connection with another human being on the fear response. Using functional magnetic resonance imaging (fMRI) to track their brain activity, Coan administered small electric shocks to sixteen married women whenever they saw an "X" flash before them. The women's brains lit up when they felt the shock and were alone. The response diminished when a stranger held their hand. It plummeted when holding the hand of their husband. The women in the happiest relationships felt the most relief.

The title of the article in the magazine for the Association for Psychological Science captures the essence of why Coan's research is important for understanding relationships: "I ~~Want~~ Need to Hold Your Hand: The Social Regulation of Emotion." The article came out after Coan's presentation on his findings at the 19th Annual APS Convention in Washington, DC. He also made a point of noting the growing body of research showing that social contact serves as a buffer between life's stressors and our health and happiness.

Trevor has observed many times in couple's counseling that strong relationships have an empowering effect on both individuals. She has counseled many successful people from high-pressure sectors such as investment banking and law and they are better off professionally when they have a strong connection with a partner. The fear factor about life in general drops precipitously.

In contrast, Trevor has also counseled several couples with infidelity issues where fear—of the relationship itself, or the spouse, or a person's self-image, and so on—is so pervasive that arousing empathy is nearly impossible. Typically, the spouse coming to grips with the partner's infidelity will sit with her arms and legs crossed in an unmistakable display of feeling threatened and wanting to keep others away. She often follows that with, "Everything's fine now. We're really having fun and doing well." At best, that's a lame speech meant to be self-soothing and make her appear less needy. At worst, it's an unconscious lie that signals a complete breakdown between her true feelings and her reality.

The key concept in using a connection with another person to reduce fear and engage the parasympathetic nervous system is *co-regulation*. Neuropsychoanalyst Allan Schore looked at attachment theory, described in chapter 2, and concluded that "attachment theory is fundamentally a regulatory theory."[25] How we attach relates to "interpersonal coordination of biological rhythms."[26]

This is a twenty-first century way of talking about creating a sense of "fear down."

"Self soothing" is an old-school approach, that is, a therapy technique based on what makes you feel good, like a bath or candlelight. "Co-dependent" and "enmeshed" are two examples of words that reflect that approach; they are dismissive of emotions and put the responsibility for feeling better solely on the individual who feels anxious, threatened or depressed. "Co-regulation" captures what is truly going on from a neuroscientific perspective.

In summary, co-regulation is how we most effectively return to a balanced, fear-down state after we've experienced fear responses. Whether that happens in the context of something like Wolpe's desensitization therapy, EFT or the exchanges of touch and caring that a couple might have, it all falls into the category of co-regulation.

FEAR: PART OF AN INTEGRATED MIND

We have been exploring the negative impact of the fear response on health, as well as ways to counter the fear response and boost the immune system. Now we will shift gears to focus on fear as an essential part of a healthy person.

Daniel J. Siegel (*The Developing Mind*) is a clinical professor of psychiatry at the University of California School of Medicine and a pioneer in defining "the mind" and "mental health." He defines the mind as "an embodied and relational process that regulates energy and information."[27] And his definition of mental health, which we will present shortly, is actually a definition of health—period.

To set the stage for his explanation, Siegel uses the hand to represent certain areas of the brain. We invite you to look at your own hand as we share his explanation.

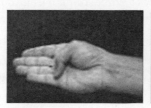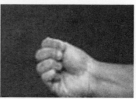

Fold your thumb onto your hand. Your thumb represents the part of your brain that processes memory and emotional reactions (the amygdala). The spinal cord is represented by the wrist and arm. The brain stem that regulates fight-flight-freeze is the lower side of the hand in the left photo. The limbic (emotion) area is the creased, center part of the hand that's underneath the thumb (the amygdala belongs to the limbic system). Think of the fingers as the cortex. The prefrontal cortex would be the tip of the fingers.

Lift the fingers up and then put them back down. Those fingertips seem to pull everything together, which is exactly what the middle prefrontal area does. As Siegel says, "It links all of the differentiated parts of the brain together. It links the cortex with the limbic area with the brain stem with the body proper and even the signals from other people's nervous systems. So the social, semantic, brain stem, limbic and cortical are all coordinated by the middle prefrontal area."[28] Based on this understanding, Siegel defines mental health as the integration of all these differentiated components.

In terms of human functioning, here is what those differentiated components represent:

1. Coordination of breathing, heart rate and other essential body operations

2. Attunement to other people, which is a feeling of being in synch and almost "inside" another person; it's the first step to compassion

3. Emotional balance, that is, experiencing emotion in your life without having it put you in a supercharged state of arousal where life becomes chaotic, or plunging you to the depths so you're depressed

4. Ability to have fear serve as a survival mechanism

5. Capacity to pause before acting; instead of ramming your car into the rear of a car that cut you off in traffic, you exercise restraint

6. Empathy or really getting inside another person's subjective experience

7. Insight—awareness of where you were in the past, where you are now and where you're going in the future

8. Morality, a sense of the greater good that takes you beyond your own personal concerns; as Siegel explains it, it's like the relationship of our organs to each other. The heart "recognizes" that if it stops pumping that will damage the lungs and so on.[29]

9. Intuition; accessing the wisdom of the body and bringing this to a conscious level

This definition of mental health illustrates that in the integration of the differentiated components, all of these nine functions are in good order. And we would suggest that if all of these functions are in good order, then you have the foundation of physical health, as well as mental health.

In chapter 9, we will look closely at how the interplay of these key functions helps define what Siegel calls the "Triangle of Well-Being."[30]

PART II

Human Nurture and Relationships

CHAPTER 4

How Society, Pop Culture and Politics Affect Your Relationships

Let's play *Jeopardy!*

The answer is: a professional basketball player, a singer, an actress, a pro football quarterback, a U.S. president, a professor of finance, a comedienne, another singer, a tennis player, a political satirist, another actress and a billionaire business magnate.

The question is: Who were a dozen of *TIME* magazine's 100 Most Influential People of 2012?

If *TIME* did correctly identify the most influential people of the day, our society felt the impact of Jeremy Lin, Rihanna, Tilda Swinton and Tim Tebow, as well as President Barack Obama and economist Andrew Lo. Our cultural genetic material now contains bits of Chelsea Handler, Adele and Novak Djokovic. If people want to know how to rise to their highest potential and join the influencers, according to *TIME*, they should closely watch and learn from Stephen Colbert, Kristen Wiig and Warren Buffett.[1]

If we were over-dramatizing the effect of such influencers on how we perceive ourselves and shape our relationships, we would all have a good laugh. The unfunny truth is that society, pop culture and politics inform us about ways of relating to one another, about the expectations associated with relationships and about what's accept-able behavior in a relationship versus what's something that elicits criticism.

As you read this chapter, ask yourself the question: Am I letting the influencers actually ruin my chances of finding connections and fulfillment because of how they affect my relationships?

MESSAGES FROM *MAD MEN*

Four messages in our advertising-infused culture work against healthy connections. In fact, the more we buy into them, the more likely we are to degrade our relationships and our health. They are:

- What you see is what you get.
- The concept of "Go West, young man!" captures a sentiment of the rogue and the loner, somehow epitomizing the best of American culture.
- Fairytales do come true.
- Porn and sexual fantasies are harmless fun.

What you see is what you get.

Society tells us whatever is on the outside is the truth—handsome, beautiful, talented, stylish or just the opposite. Don't jump to conclu-sions about the sources of those messages, though. It isn't just media that reinforces our focus on the superficial. Without even meaning to, parents and pastors can "train" children to project virtue by hiding their vices; they look like "good" people, even when they hop over to the other side of the moral fence.

A humorous part of Hollywood lore is how many fine actresses weren't taken seriously until they "uglified" themselves for a role. *What you see is what you get* had condemned them, at least to some extent, to the perception that their primary value to movies was their attractiveness. Charlize Theron, Halle Berry, Nicole Kidman and Hilary Swank (who did it twice) are among the beautiful actresses who forced us to look past their pretty surface and they won Academy Awards for it.

In terms of relationships, keeping our attention on externals does to our friendships and other love relationships what Hollywood ostensibly did to those actresses: prevents them from giving us their best and blocks us from knowing what depth they have to offer.

A friend of Maryann's joined a dating website and began trolling for tall, trashy blondes (that's his description, not ours). In consideration of some of the non-physical traits he'd listed as desirable, he was matched with a petite brunette who happened to be a well-educated single mother and a fabulous cook. As he sat across the table from her on their first date, his inner voice screamed, "She is *not* what I want." But he's a polite guy and wasn't going to just walk out on the date. That was ten years ago and they're still together. When we hear stories like this, we get the urge to hug the people who design the software for some of these dating sites. How many people put their faith in the matching capabilities and ended up in a strong relationship with someone who looked nothing like the person they thought they wanted?

That was the case for Craig and Janie, who fell in love at first e-mail. Craig was always frail. He wanted a connection, but women would meet him and see that he looked emaciated and always seemed to be in pain. He went on one of the relationship sites seven years ago and met Janie. They were matched by interests, values and geography. They e-mailed. They talked on the phone. He said, "I'm sickly and frail." She said, "I'm overweight and strong." They both loved children and married within months of their first phone conversation. Three years later, they had twin girls, who are now nearly four years old. Just after celebrating his daughters' third birthday, Craig found out he had bone cancer. Not long ago, he died. But he was happy, and his whole family celebrated the connection he'd made with Janie and the beautiful children they had produced.

If Craig and Janie had met at a party or at a bar, they wouldn't have looked twice at each other. By getting to know each other on the basis of values and interests, they fell in love, sight unseen. Their relationship sustained his life far longer than any medicine would have.

In his book, *Situations Matter: Understanding How Context Transforms Your World*, social psychology researcher Sam Sommers notes that we tend to take our context for granted and in doing so, we often accept that what we see is what we get. We like to minimize the amount of effort it takes to make decisions, and make snap judgments about people because it just takes less brain power.[2]

In her body language classes, Maryann stresses the importance of considering context in reading body language and this emphasis often surprises her audiences, who assume that particular gestures can always be interpreted a certain way. In other words, some of them came to the workshop wanting "the secret code," and didn't realize that reading body language involves a good deal of watching and analyzing. She first poses the question, "What do crossed arms signify?" The usual response is "a way of keeping people away, a barrier." The truth is, without knowing something about context, it's nearly impossible to be certain what the crossed arms mean. The person could be cold, afraid, trying to show arrogance or disdain or maybe just has arms that are so long that crossing them makes him feel less conspicuous.

The Grant Study provides hard evidence that focusing on externals does not serve us well in terms of achievement or relationships. It bolsters what we asserted at the beginning of chapter 3, which is that the positive physical effects of a secure relationship do powerful and practical things for our bodies and our sense of risk-taking and competence. The Grant Study began in 1938 and involved two populations of white males, one of which was a group of 268 Harvard University students. The research team did bi-annual follow-up through questionnaires, information from participants' physicians and personal interviews, and kept track of participants still living until they were well into their nineties.

New York Times columnist David Brooks focused on one aspect of the Grant Study in an article entitled "The Heart Grows Stronger."

"In the 1930s and 1940s, the researchers didn't pay much attention to the men's relationships. Instead, following the intellectual fashions of the day, they paid a lot of attention

*to the men's physiognomy. Did they have a "mascu-
line" body type? Did they show signs of vigorous genetic
endowments?*

*"But as this study — the Grant Study — progressed,
the power of relationships became clear. The men who grew
up in homes with warm parents were much more likely to
become first lieutenants and majors in World War II. The
men who grew up in cold, barren homes were much more
likely to finish the war as privates.*

*"Body type was useless as a predictor of how the men
would fare in life. So was birth order or political affilia-
tion. Even social class had a limited effect. But having a
warm childhood was powerful. As George Vaillant, the
study director, sums it up in "Triumphs of Experience," his
most recent summary of the research, 'It was the capacity
for intimate relationships that predicted flourishing in all
aspects of these men's lives.'"[3]*

Even with the preponderance of evidence reminding us to look
past externals, we look for easy ways to understand each other and
ourselves time after time. Externals do tell us something about people,
but generally, they are like the proverbial tip of the iceberg: only 15 to
20 percent of the total.

The quality of our relationships is what affects our health and
well-being and that is not shaped by whether or not someone has
made a fashion faux pas or pays for dinner with a gold credit card.

One of the facts that surfaced through the years in the Grant
Study is that, as Brooks suggests in the title of the piece, the hearts
of the men assumed more significance in their health and happiness
than their looks or degrees. They found that being the rogue or loner
was a miserable way to live—that is, those who actually did live to
realize it. Brooks makes it abundantly clear what happened to the others: "Of the 31 men in the study incapable of establishing intimate
bonds, only four are still alive. Of those who were better at forming
relationships, more than a third are living."[4]

Sometimes it is important to stay strong and be tough, but to take it to an extreme and go it alone when you need help wears you down. The Grant Study affirms that. Many people, particularly men, are schooled to not even have empathy with themselves, to ignore pain and be driven to succeed no matter what. It's culturally more acceptable for women to ask for help; women are less inclined to judge each other as "needy" when it comes to relationships. Even so, men need relationships/connections just as much as women; however, our society doesn't support their "neediness."

The concept of "Go West, young man!" captures a sentiment of the rogue and the loner, somehow epitomizing the best of American culture.

Modern men tend to suffer from this myth more than women, but many of us who grew up with the women's movement message that we could do anything men could do let the myth affect our behavior as well. And because we associate self-sufficiency with values, we tend to view entrepreneurial spirit and lone-cowboy behavior as somehow inherently moral.

When golf star Jack Nicklaus campaigned for Mitt Romney in the 2012 presidential election, he hit hard on the theme of restoring America's greatness by encouraging—no, insisting on—self-reliance. He espoused the view, consistent with Romney's, that people succeed primarily by virtue of their own efforts. Making the message personal, he said he chose golf as his profession because it didn't require teamwork: "I didn't lean on somebody else in tough times."[5]

In fact, he misspoke. When Nicklaus hit a slump in the late 1970s, two men who were friends and coaches came to his aid and helped him fix his full swing and short game. Maybe he didn't "lean on them," but he clearly needed them. This example illustrates that we may remember times of triumph that may have felt like individual victories but there was always a parent, coach, friend or someone else to whom we felt connected who helped us attain our goal in some way.

The truth of humanity is that, sometimes, you can't carry your own weight.

When Maryann was in the first Eco-Challenge, a ten-day, 376-mile adventure race over long stretches of desert, mountains and icy canyon water, she got a respiratory infection. For a day, she could barely breathe, much less carry a forty-five-pound backpack. Her four male teammates offered to split up the contents of the pack so she wouldn't have any weight to carry. She protested, "I can carry it myself." After all, she didn't want to be dependent on a bunch of guys. She soon learned the difference between self-sufficiency and selfishness; if she didn't let them carry her pack, they'd never make it to the next checkpoint in time and their team would be out of the race.

Almost no one is immune to this. However, most of us are taught to be so self-sufficient that we sometimes don't even notice that someone has made a kind and caring gesture. Trevor's producer on her radio show offered to make her coffee recently and she said, "No, that's okay." He knew she wanted a cup of coffee, though, so he pressed the issue: "You mean you don't want me to take care of you?" So she told him the truth: "I'd love a cup of coffee. Thank you." Just saying that gave her a kind of internal melt, an easing of tension that transformed her mood.

A 2011 study done by the School of Nursing at the University of Rochester demonstrated that survival rates among male cardiac patients with partners noticeably exceeded those of single men. Certainly, one could jump to the conclusion that men in a relationship had a better chance of growing stronger because they received more support at home in making changes in diet and exercise. That's only part of the story, however. The study concluded:

> *In fact, marital status was a better predictor of long-term survival after bypass surgery than traditional heart-disease risk factors like smoking, high blood pressure, diabetes, and prior heart attacks. And the benefit may be true for anyone in a long-term, supportive relationship, married or not.*[6]

"Are American Friendships Superficial?" Jeffrey M. Fish, a contributor to *Psychology Today*, asked. The conclusion was "yes and no," and part of the "yes" analysis stated: "American individualism means that we give more emphasis to our own needs in forming and dissolving relationships than do cultures organized around traditional forms and relationships."[7] We are not advocating abandoning that individualism, but rather weaving it into an appreciation for connection and tribe that goes deeper than wearing the same jersey to a football game.

We may be seeing signs of change with younger generations of men, but the research isn't there yet. A question to pose is this: Is social networking, in fact, good for young men because it encourages the *concept* of connection, even though the method of connection might seem flawed? The desire for people to be in touch is the important, human impulse behind using our devices to text, post updates and e-mail.

Fairytales do come true.

The marriage of Kate Middleton and Prince William of Great Britain captivated the world. Millions of Americans rose early that day to watch a commoner suddenly become a member of the royal family. We could collectively sigh, "See? Fairytales do come true!" Some in the United States had let that sigh out nearly five years prior when Katie Holmes married Hollywood royalty Tom Cruise, the man she'd had a crush on as a child. These relationships seem to validate our not-so-secret belief that make-believe stories like those seen in movies like *Pretty Woman* and *Titanic* happen all the time. The nation is full of beautiful, good-hearted hookers who become the love of a handsome dealmaker's life; there are all kinds of voluptuous young women who would gladly trade financial security, and even their very lives, for romance with a poor artist.

In those modern fairytales, there is always an initial power imbalance rooted in money that seems to magically dissipate—at least for a while—because of "true love," which would not take shape, of course, unless both parties were incredibly attractive.

We drill the fairytale mentality into our little girls from an early age, as Peggy Orenstein, well-known for writing about issues affecting women and girls, notes in *Cinderella Ate My Daughter*. Orenstein was shocked when her daughter seemed transformed after a week of pre-school: "She came home having memorized, as if by osmosis, all the names and gown colors of the Disney princesses."[8] Her daughter also developed a thirst for pink, from dresses to a Magic 8-ball. But the worst part was the messages about what to *be*: "And what was the first thing that culture told her about being a girl? Not that she was competent, strong, creative, or smart, but that every little girl wants—or should want—to be the Fairest of Them All."[9]

This was the advice given to Trevor's daughter from a high school friend of hers: "You don't need to learn math because you'll marry a guy who'll pay the bills." Would she have said that if she considered Trevor's daughter unattractive?

This sentiment is so pervasive that some version of it makes its way into the minds of little girls all over the country (and perhaps beyond). A 2012 report from the Women's Media Center delivers stark statistics confirming that women still tend to be "hyper-sexualized" a great deal of the time and that female characters in television "are more likely to have an undefined employment status" than male characters.[10] We're still grappling with media images of women who seem to get the fairytale ending they want, or at least have a shot at it, on the basis of their looks and not how they choose to contribute to society.

As a corollary, a single woman in many modern societies is often depicted as someone who needs a man, but not in the healthy way we've talked about elsewhere in this book. That need helps shapes the transactional nature of many relationships—a subject discussed in the upcoming section of this chapter.

When we buy into any aspect of the fairytale ending approach to connections, we exacerbate the kind of pressures and expectations that are really hard on relationships. The concept of "happily ever after" is absurd outside of a cartoon princess marriage. There will be joyful days and painful days.

On some level we all know this but we encourage the media to show an anti-fairytale view in ways that teach us nothing about relationships or how to grow emotionally. Through reality TV, we ask for glimpses of the fortunate lives of rich and beautiful people; the shows allow us to insert ourselves into those worlds filled with material advantages. As much as the lives of the women on "Big Rich Atlanta" and "Keeping Up with the Kardashians" are projected as full of privilege and opportunity, what we choose to capture as the "reality" of their day-to-day existence is often the backbiting, vengeful, overly dramatic interactions. We don't want them to be happy because they have so much stuff—why should they have happiness and strong relationships, too?

The authentic reality is that celebrities like Kim Kardashian and Kanye West want to be loved for who they are, too. They need that as much as we do. And no matter what we might think, their rarified lives don't guarantee that connection; they actually make it harder to achieve.

Even as a little girl, Judith wanted to marry a doctor. When her friends asked, "Why?" she would say, "They do something worthwhile and they're smart!"

After graduating from a prestigious women's college, Judith returned to New York and secured a position as an art historian in a museum. She met Stephen, an anesthesiologist, at a party with mutual friends and married him a year later. Her life with Stephen seemed like a dream come true.

Judith pared down her hours at the museum after her first child was born. After the birth of their third, she stopped working completely. She also experienced, alternately, feelings of depression and agitation, partially because she felt distanced from the raising of her own children. Stephen's style of parenting dominated in the household; she was expected to agree with the way he indulged the children. He overrode all of her decisions regarding discipline.

Seeing her mood swings, Stephen sent her to one of his colleagues in psychiatry who prescribed mood-stabilizing drugs.

By the time the children were teenagers, they either bullied their mother or were dismissive of her. Judith started to experience occasional pains that curtailed her physical activities and she was prone to injuring herself. At the slightest irritation, like the toaster dying while she was trying to make a bagel for breakfast, she exploded, slamming her fist onto the counter and screaming at the top of her lungs.

Stephen's physician friend strengthened her prescription and, for her aches and pains, sent her to another doctor who prescribed a painkiller.

She continued a downward spiral physically and mentally—all the while interpreting the top-notch medical care she thought she was getting as loving gestures by her husband. The sicker she got, the more he seemed to care about her. Even the children seemed to soften a bit as they saw her able to do less and less.

Judith had come from a home with loving but very exacting parents. They expected her to perform well in school and to excel in swimming, a sport for which she seemed to have tremendous natural ability. The only time they let her rest was when she had the usual childhood illnesses or one time when she broke her arm.

Stephen came from a large family with parents who had a hard time giving adequate time to all the kids. He developed a role within the family as the one to go to for comfort and caring. Making his siblings feel better gave him a real sense of value. Later on when he became a doctor, his success in life was centered on sick and injured people. When he was around people with health issues, he was in his element. And when his wife started manifesting symptoms of various kinds, oddly enough, he felt more connected to her.

Stephen had no intention of being horrible to his wife; he felt he gave her and the children his best. Judith went into the marriage with nothing wrong with her organically but fell into a pattern of sickness, and it's highly likely because people around her would pay attention to her and take care of her.

In-laws on both sides pointed fingers: "He's killing her with those drugs!" "She's a nutcase who's ruining his life and traumatizing their children!"

The fact is, they may both be getting what they want out of the marriage. It may not be emotionally or physically healthy, but it's what they want. They are managing a level of intimacy in a transactional way and it's just too much of a good fit for them to change it.

If you view things through an attachment lens, you stop blaming or judging. There is a deeper meaning than right or wrong. People have a normal tendency to look for the black and white, to pick a side and say, "This one is righteous and that one is wicked." In fact, people function in ways we can't necessarily understand and people in a relationship like Stephen and Judith's do not benefit from having us judge them. But make no mistake about it: We are not talking about relationships where someone (or both) is clearly abusive.

In Stephen's framework, he is a loving, caring person. In Judith's, she is someone in need of loving and caring. They each stepped into the other's fairytale and assumed their roles.

Another version of the fairytale—the male-centric one—has been poisoned by the severe downturn in the economy that struck in 2008. Many young men who were raised in a comfortable environment have resentment welling up because of the "mancession," defined as an economic circumstance "in which the unemployment rate is substantially higher among men than it is among women."[11] Their fathers had reliable, and possibly lucrative, employment but these young men found themselves with nobody saying, "Oh, you're Joe's son! C'mon and take that corner office."

And while predictability in opportunity for men was shrinking, during the height of the recession in 2008-2009 American women earned about 60 percent of college degrees.[10] They are powering up into leadership roles in all sectors of the economy; many young women are eclipsing their male counterparts.

As a result, a great number of twenty-something men are demoralized by their lack of success and even bitter about women doing slightly better than they are in the workforce. Demoralized, bitter men have a serious handicap in cultivating healthy connections, in which the ability to feel vulnerable with another person is essential. They feel as though society has already made them feel so vulnerable and emasculated that they are desperate to display some power. All around them are plenty of tools to display power: electronic gadgets, guns and cars. They may also turn to verbal and/or physical abuse of someone they've "hooked up" with. Not only do they move farther and farther away from the fairytale life of success, but they also reduce their chances of developing a normal, secure attachment with someone in an intimate relationship.

There are those who plunge into the good life by finding women who offer them the comfortable lifestyle they assumed they would have. They accept a financial imbalance in the relationship without considering how that can easily translate into a power imbalance— something that naturally emphasizes the transactional aspects of the relationship rather than the emotional aspects. A man Trevor knows was formerly married to an extremely wealthy woman. Her father, Joe Smithton, was the head of a Fortune 500 company. The friend said he lost his identity while married to Susie. At parties or any other gathering, he would hear both direct and side references to him as "Joe Smithton's son-in-law." He says that his own name just stopped being relevant.

Porn and sexual fantasies are harmless fun.

Many feel that pornography and sexual fantasies can be positive, satisfying additions to lovemaking and sexual play in the context of a secure relationship. Unfortunately, porn tends to be enjoyed in a way that damages the self-esteem of women and may even increase the likelihood that they will be the victims of aggressive behavior. Similarly, sexual fantasies can put distance between two people and/or make one of them feel inadequate or afraid instead of bringing them together for some lighthearted fun.

Currently, Americans spend nearly fifty dollars per capita per year on pornography and this amount is even greater in some other countries, such as China and Japan.[11] The American porn industry is reportedly raking in more than $13 billion a year.[12] That's roughly twice the 2013 budget of the National Science Foundation[13] and about one-third more than the 2013 budget for the Centers for Disease Control and Prevention (CDC).[14]

New studies that suggest that porn is bad for a relationship circle around this fact: Pornography contributes to violence against women.[15]

Lots of studies on the effect of pornography have seemed to contradict each other, so Paul Wright, an Indiana University professor who does research on sex in the media, relied on meta-analyses to draw his conclusion. Meta-analysis is the study of studies; it involves analyzing data from multiple studies to determine if there's a preponderance of evidence in one direction or another. Wright concluded that exposure to both violent pornography and nonviolent pornography increased the probability of subsequent aggression.[16]

On the issue of sexual fantasies, attachment styles seem to affect them, according to Susan Krauss Whitbourne, a professor of psychology at the University of Massachusetts and author of *The Search for Fulfillment*. And when these fantasies offer the sense of connection and satisfaction that the relationship itself ought to be providing, they can distance the daydreamers from the real issues of the relationship. She asserts that:

> *Anxiously attached people, then, are more likely to equate sex with love, especially when they feel that things aren't going well with their partner. In their fantasies, they see themselves as being humiliated and helpless at the hands of a powerful partner. Avoidantly attached people do just the opposite. On bad days, their fantasies take the form of escapism, hostility, and emotional detachment. In their minds, if not in their behavior, they were the ones most likely to walk out on their partner on days when they weren't getting along well.*[17]

Anxiously-attached people might well rely on sex rather than a genuine connection with another human being to meet their needs to feel safe and secure. But they might also use money, drugs, alcohol or even their own children. The commonality is their anxiety around not having whatever "it" is. It can manifest as an addiction to a substance, or an addiction to a lifestyle or situation. In all cases, "it" makes you feel better for a short period of time—secure, safe and self-satisfied. But "it" is neither a route toward a secure attachment, nor is it a substitute for a genuine connection.

The repeated exposure to porn or the reliance on sexual fantasies for these anxiously or avoidantly-attached people is *harmful* fun, regardless of what "open-minded" pop culture messages they may hear.

RELATIONSHIPS DEFINED BY TRANSACTIONS

On New Year's Day of 2013, an off-duty police officer shot and killed a bull elk in Boulder, Colorado, where the elk was a sort of neighborhood pet that grazed on their crab apples. Many citizens were shocked at the unprovoked killing and staged a vigil. Several days later, *Denver Post* columnist Rich Tosches aimed his wit at the vigil participants. After all, he joked, Native Americans called it *wapiti*, which he said was "a combination of the Native words wa ('who') and piti ('ate all my shrubs?')."[18] (For the record, wapiti means "white rump.") He obviously thought it was hilarious that people got together to sing songs and light candles just because some lumbering thing that was half-trophy, half-stew took a bullet.

What Tosches mocked was a display of compassion—compassion is the human characteristic that runs counter to the transactional aspect of relationships. The transactional view of the elk situation is this: We, the residents of this Boulder community, let you roam around unencumbered and allowed you to eat whatever you wanted. Now it's your turn to give us something we want—your antlers, your meat and your hide. The compassion-based view of the situation is this: We, the residents of this Boulder community, willingly shared our neighborhood with you and you owed us nothing. We enjoyed your presence and are sad because your life ended so brutally.

If you speak of relationships in a transactional way, you focus on them as you would a business deal.

Ted, a client of Trevor's colleague, noted that the only reason he was willing to come in and try couple's counseling is that he was really afraid of losing his lifestyle if he and his wife, Wendy, split up. Wendy is a classic, over-functioning, blaming-pursuer who earns a lot of money—much more than he does. Ted is a withdrawer whose small business would have collapsed without her financial assistance.

She wanted to go straight to the transactional aspect of what was wrong with the relationship. It would be easy for most people to jump right in there with her, but it's important to realize that it's who they are as a connected pair that demands the focus—not the "right" or "wrong" of the transactions.

In her view, she makes it possible for them to have financial abundance, so he ought to pull his weight at home: make the kids' sandwiches, do the laundry and sweep out the garage. Wendy is stuck in the societal norm that allows her to establish what he should do for her and how he should do it because she generates stability and prosperity through her earnings. That's the deal. Ted can't live up to her standards—when he makes the sandwiches, does the laundry or sweeps out the garage, he does it "wrong"—so he gives up and doesn't do any of the chores.

This transactional orientation goes back to her childhood, with a father who always pushed himself and everyone else to do "more." That is, there was no ability to *be*; one always had to *do*. In a relationship centered on doing, there's a lot of anxiety when things don't get done.

When that childhood experience came up in therapy, it was an "ah-ha!" moment for both of them. Ted finally understood the underpinning of Wendy's behavior, and she understood herself a lot better. When she wasn't doing something, she felt insecure; it had never occurred to her to turn to her husband and say, "I'm anxious. Help me out!" He cried, expressed his love for her and said, "I'm here for you." They both took an emotional step toward each other—the first, tentative step toward nurturing compassion and suppressing the transactional aspect of their marriage.

Our societal endorsement of a transactional mentality might be linked to our Western appreciation for causality, that is, a cause-and-effect relationship. It's very much a part of our philosophical tradition. Wendy and Ted had defined their relationship by activity X leading to response Y. Neither one of them saw the innate value of their relationship, apart from the give-and-take they had established.

This transactional mentality probably affects most relationships in a negative way—at least some of the time. There are many couples in which the husband truly believes that his generosity in allowing his wife unlimited use of the American Express card has earned him a blow job at least once a week. In therapy, they question, "Why doesn't she get it? That's part of the bargain." Another, more common way this might play out is when one partner has to work and so the other one needs to pick up the kids at school. Later on, the partner who picked up the kids feels as though he has a "credit" in the relationship: "I did this, so now you should do that for me."

All kinds of media, from romantic comedies to songs, often have the built-in assumption that a relationship revolves around some set of transactions. Some couples even negotiate having and raising children. Certainly there are practical, transactional elements to family life; however, the heart of the process should be love, not who does what.

Carol had an advanced degree in musicology as well as a law degree from Stanford University. Her whole life had been a series of super-achievements. Right after she made partner at her law firm, she found out she was pregnant. Her husband, Charlie, was a computer programmer.

She laid down some rules if he wanted her to have this baby: While she was pregnant and not consuming alcohol, he couldn't consume alcohol. When she went to bed, she expected him to go to bed. He also had to go to every check-up with her. And after the baby was born, he would quit his job and freelance from home so she could return to work.

Charlie agreed to the terms. Two years into the arrangement, he agreed to the terms again when she became pregnant with their second child. After the kids were both in school, Carol told Charlie he could go back to work, but by that time, he enjoyed the flexibility of working from home. He also really enjoyed playing a favorite video game without the interruption of kids.

Charlie had an avoidant attachment style. He also spun himself into a cycle of shame, feeling cultural pressure to support his family, yet not being as capable as his wife of doing so. Carol added to his sense of inferiority by figuratively keeping him under her boot. Online role-playing games actually made him feel capable and powerful; when he played them, he felt good about himself. Carol's focus on checks and balances—never slowing down to feel the humanity of the marriage— fueled Charlie's cycle of shame and kept increasing the distance between them. In a relationship infected with the perspective that money is power, one person emerges as self-righteous, putting the other one down. The ability for empathic responses shuts down.

Carol had never had a secure attachment to herself; she was anxiously attached and felt "safe" only when pushing herself to the max. Given that she couldn't show compassion for herself, she certainly had no capacity to show it for Charlie. She set him up in an apartment and filed for divorce. She saw him as a bad investment: he hadn't kept up his end of the transactional relationship.

Breakthroughs can occur for couples like this. Sometimes, they start to refocus when the self-righteous person just takes the time to ask a simple question. Instead of making a blaming statement—"You spend all your time playing that game!"—Carol and Charlie might have made headway if she had asked, "Why do you play that video game?" and then really listened to the response.

WHAT'S "BREAKING UP?"

The song "Breaking Up Is Hard to Do" was popular in the 1970s (the second version, not the first one from the 1960s). Many people in their mid-thirties and younger would find the sentiment in the song quaint and reminiscent of a time when couples dated. They were young people who, when they stopped dating, went through some angst and "broke up." But if you were born after 1980, it's likely you belong to a hook-up culture rather than a dating culture.

Today many young adults don't ask each other on dates. They text each other at the last minute. Instead of asking on a Wednesday if someone is available Saturday night for dinner, someone sends a text announcing, "I'm @ d bar W f? cum ovr."

Trevor's stepdaughter, now in her twenties, told her that she had friends in college who thought they had a boyfriend until summer vacation rolled around. The girls brought up the discussion of "what next." Their conversation went something like this:

> **Her:** "Are we going to continue to go out this summer?"
> **Him:** "What do you mean 'go out'? We weren't going out."
> **Her:** "We've been seeing each other since September."
> **Him:** "We were just hooking up."

The name for their experiences together is not dating; it's called "consistent hooking up."

Fast forward to when these young adults are in their mid-twenties or thirties. They still don't know how to date, that is, there is no more ritualized courtship with the question "Is this going anywhere?" threaded throughout the experience. And ending an ongoing hook-up is not "breaking up;" it is merely a matter of stopping the texts. There is no need to feel the disappointment, anger or drama of a breakup. It may still happen for one of the parties, but it probably won't be an experience that the two of them share. Nonetheless, at some point, biology will take over and the hook-up generation will want to create families. Focusing on the "now" of a connection may end up being a very uncomfortable, if not daunting, exercise after years of asynchronous communication through texting and social media.

THE SHAME OF SHAME

We publicly shame the celebrities who don't live up to the "truth" about themselves, for example, a fashion faux pas by someone with a reputation for impeccable taste. Cleverly written, stinging criticisms entertain us online and on television. We look forward to the wit of a take-down like "She appears to be wearing a bikini cover-up that came free in a bag of Cheetos."[19]

We don't want to desecrate the fine literary tradition of trashing bad taste, but the fact is that human beings don't have emotions in a vacuum except for shame (unless we are seriously avoidant). Emotions bring others to us, whereas shame isolates. So why do we do this to the people we supposedly idolize?

We keep people in line with shame, but over-shaming children or adults, celebrities or our next-door neighbor is a horrible thing. Shame makes a person feel less worthy, less lovable. People who are shamed tend to pull away.

It's extremely rare in our society to rise above this, but a remarkable Sikh woman triggered exactly that response. After being mocked online for her unusually thick facial hair, her response elicited the unthinkable: the twenty-year-old Floridian who first ridiculed her apologizing to a global audience for being "ignorant." Unlike many people, who would allow shame to block compassion for themselves and others, she had the emotional strength to brush aside debilitating shame. Instead, she turned it into an opportunity for connection and education. Here is what she said:

> *Hey, guys. This is Balpreet Kaur, the girl from the picture. I actually didn't know about this until one of my friends told on Facebook. If the OP wanted a picture, they could have just asked and I could have smiled :) However, I'm not embarrassed or even humiliated by the attention [negative and positive] that this picture is getting because, it's who I am. Yes, I'm a baptized Sikh woman with facial hair. Yes, I realize that my gender is often confused and I look different from most women. However, baptized Sikhs believe in the*

sacredness of this body—it is a gift that has been given to us
by the Divine Being [which is genderless, actually] and we
must keep it intact as a submission to the divine will.

...By transcending societal views of beauty, I believe
that I can focus more on my actions. My attitude and
thoughts and actions have more value in them than my
body because I recognize that this body is just going to be-
come ash in the end, so why fuss about it? When I die, no
one is going to remember what I looked like, heck, my kids
will forget my voice and slowly, all physical memory will
fade away. However, my impact and legacy will remain
and, by not focusing on the physical beauty, I have time to
cultivate those inner virtues and hopefully, focus my life
on creating change and progress for this world in any way
I can.[20]

Typically, shaming like that heaped on Balpreet Kaur is toxic.
Just look at how many suicides of juveniles have occurred within
recent years because of shame/bullying like she received. A significant difference is her secure attachment style. Spiritual faith can be a
strong and healthy attachment, as in this case.

Our acceptance of being nasty to one another, of provoking a
sense of shame, runs deep in our society. Reality television thrives on
the concept of "info-shamement." Political conversations are fueled by
shaming the opposition, with our choice as voters sometimes coming
down to "who seems to deserve less shaming?"

Prior to politically and socially pointed comedies such as *All in*
the Family, network television featured comedies with their roots in
interpersonal issues rather than societal ones. They featured typical,
middle-class life events. One example is the episode of *Ozzie and*
Harriet that involved their vertically-challenged son going to the
prom with a tall girl. By the 1970s, several comedies covered issues
of "shame" like abortion or poverty. They got their laughs out of
shaming people—embarrassing them. This is a practice that has
continued uninterrupted in the media.

Within a couple, shame can cause a backlash that triggers behavior that can destroy a union. It isn't uncommon for the shamed individual to seek affairs in retaliation. For example, Gary married his college sweetheart, Sally, a woman of extraordinary beauty as well as wealth. Her mother had been a renowned actress who was quite frugal. Their first few years together seemed wonderful, with his middle-class background not having much bearing on their day-to-day life. But through the years, he had a growing sense of being "less than" and occasionally he felt that Sally was humiliating him by reminding him in front of her celebrity pals that she had status and money.

He worked hard and earned a decent income, but that was nothing compared to her seemingly bottomless well of investments and cash.

After nearly twenty years of marriage, he started seeing prostitutes, and ultimately, found a favorite. In his mind, he was in love with her. In actuality, the balance of power in their relationship was something he enjoyed: He gave her money and she gave him gratitude, respect and sex. He had no shame in her presence, no sense of being judged.

By the time the affair started, he had amassed a small fortune, since his daily living expenses were covered by his wife's money. At one point, he admitted to giving the woman an extra $1,000 a month for her rent. Sally didn't even seem ruffled at first. Sally simply ordered him to stop with the tone of an annoyed boss who had no time for such foolishness.

Gary persisted, and in an odd way of taking a stand, he gave the hooker a lump sum of $100,000. It was his money, theoretically his to spend as he pleased. Sally may have often looked down her nose at him, making him feel insignificant and ridiculous, but the hooker made him feel like a superhero. In his mind, the act also turned him into a philanthropist since he gave the hooker the money so she could go to school and get out of the business.

Sally refused to give up on him and the marriage. They delved into couple's counseling and even had separate sessions to try to resolve the underlying issues in the relationship.

Away from his wife, Gary spoke more fluently. He seemed like a different person and he actually took on an aura that made him seem quite attractive. In contrast, when he was around Sally he was awkward and on edge.

One of the therapeutic challenges was clearly to help them excise shame from their relationship. It took a near catastrophe to do it. Gary had a serious health scare and Sally stayed by his side and nursed him, day after day. Shame and blame found themselves replaced by compassion. By hiring people for around-the-clock care, she could have kept him and his illness at arm's length. Instead, she stepped up emotionally. It's too soon to tell whether or not this episode will have a transformative effect, but the experience of genuine compassion often does.

UPRISINGS FROM THE INNER CIRCLE

The Very Rev. Gary Hall, dean of the Washington National Cathedral, announced in early 2013 that his church would begin hosting same-sex weddings—and his description of the advantages for heterosexual couples contained marvelous insights about healthy, secure relationships. In an interview with National Public Radio's Melissa Block, he noted how the new ceremony might open some minds about the way members of a couple view each other:

Hall: One of the things I think that same-sex marriage has to teach straight people is about the possibility of a totally equal and mutual relationship before God. Our marriage service that's in our prayer book—which, you know, has been revised several times since 1549—carries with it the vestiges of a patriarchal society, so…

Block: How so?

Hall: So, well, you know, for example, handing the bride over to the groom; the vows in the prayer book, up until 1928, were love, honor and obey for the woman. As much as we've tried to revise our marriage service to make everything equal and mutual, it still has with it some connotations and vestiges of pre-modern ways of understanding male-female relationships.

I think one of the ways in which gay and lesbian couples really can teach something to straight couples is the way in which they hold up the possibility of an absolute equality and mutuality in marriage. And so this new rite, it's entirely different than the old marriage service. It's really grounded in baptism, and the idea of a radical equality of all people in Christ and before God.[21]

One way to summarize Hall's appreciation for same-sex vows is how they spotlight the kind of balance, mutual respect and shared vulnerability that characterize secure relationships.

Other influencers in society are also coming into the light of the media to make an effort to change the emphasis from anxious and avoidant behavior to a more secure style. For example, former Republican Governor Jon Huntsman and Democratic Senator Joe Manchin are gaining some traction with their No Labels movement, the purpose of which is to change governmental attitudes about how to make laws and work together.[22] No Labels is another faint, yet hopeful, sign that people in the United States are sick—literally—over the shaming, blaming and power plays that our society, pop culture and politics now depict as a normal part of our relationships.

We don't think it's either wise or fair to suggest that the breakdown of ritualized courtship and the use of technology to connect is all bad news. Some of the biggest influences in our culture are the younger generations. They are trying to make relationships work while integrating a lot of new tools into their lives. Maybe the uprising from that "inner circle" will be making a habit of reaching out to other people—often without any agenda.

CHAPTER 5

How Your Upbringing Shapes Your Connections

The way your upbringing impacts your connections isn't a simple matter of, "He married a woman who's just like his mother!" or "She chose a partner who treats her like her dad treated her." Much of this has to do with the ways that memory and language take shape as we develop. Our primary caregivers, who are often parents, have a great impact on that but so do peers and teachers.

Much of the discussion centers on attachment styles, which can be expressed as the ways we relate to the world and other people. As we've suggested before, certain styles of attachment are associated with chronic stress in our lives and that endangers our bodies.

The condition of our physical and mental health is intimately related to the way we attach to other beings. Knowing more about how these attachment styles developed can give us tremendous insights into identifying ours and then consciously making changes to improve our relationships and health.

Even though attachment styles develop when we are young, they are active throughout our lives.

WHO WAS THERE FOR YOU?

From the time you enter the world, you exist somewhere between danger and safety, sometimes entering completely into one territory or the other. When you feel safe and secure, your guard is down and you connect easily with other people so that you can relax with and even enjoy your vulnerability as a human being.

In the opposite situation, the freeze-fight-flight condition we described in chapter 3, the amygdala jumps into action, processing information much faster than the thinking brain, and you immediately look for a route back to safety. If somebody whom you normally feel stress-free with is nearby, that person becomes part of your "solution" to the threat. It's called "proximity seeking behavior." These are people with whom you have some kind of trusted connection; they are the ones who help you regulate your responses to a threat and, ultimately, calm down.

When John Bowlby did his seminal work on attachment theory, he focused on the interaction of children with their caregivers. Bowlby found that the nature of that interaction affected the health of the children. They needed to know that the caregiver was there for them and that the caregiver would respond to them. The "still face" experiment referred to in chapter 1 relates to that second component of the interaction.

The people in a child's life who affect health and well-being—and, as a corollary, the person's attachment style—may include parents, boyfriends/girlfriends of parents, stepparents, grandparents, brothers and sisters, nannies, pastors, teachers, pediatricians, therapists and anyone else who has regular influence over the emotional and physical life of the child.

In 1974, Ann Lewin-Benham, the author of five books on learning, founded the Capital Children's Museum (now known as the National Children's Museum) in an area of Washington, DC, that had been hit hard by race riots and poverty. There were lots of latchkey kids, so she immediately launched a program to give them a place to come for activities and meals after school. The program that she created involved senior citizens in the area who came to the museum every day to be with the children. It didn't take long for them to become "grandparents" to them. The senior citizens had some effect on the children's emotional growth. A program like that engenders relationships that can become critical in the way children develop trust in others and how safe they feel in their environments.

Sometimes a family cultivates such strong and trusting bonds among all its members that the idea of "one big happy family" really does come to life. In other words, secure attachments formed for everyone in the household, because everyone was there for each other. One story that epitomizes this experience involves two sisters who were nuns together as well as life-long friends. Sister Jean Marie Wheeler and Sister Elaine Wheeler were ninety-eight and ninety-six when they passed away one day apart, on January 17 and 18 of 2013. They served their final years together in an upstate New York convent. They had three other sisters who also became nuns and all five of them taught and lived in the Albany area most of their lives. Two other sisters did not join convents; they married and had children. The siblings remained close from childhood until death.[1]

In answering the question, "who was there for you?" you should begin to consider all the people who played significant and positive roles in your survival and your emotional life as a child. They are the people who made you feel safe and gave you reasons to trust them. In answering the opposite question, "who was *not* there for you?" you will begin to understand who might have contributed to a style of attachment that wouldn't be characterized—at least not all the time—as secure.

HOW ATTACHMENT STYLES DEVELOP

Attachment styles reflect your view of yourself as well as your view of other people.

Earlier in this chapter, we addressed the way people can help us regulate our responses to danger. If we're young and helpless, and there is rarely someone there who provides safe haven, then stress becomes a day-to-day, moment-by-moment reality. If mommy, daddy or big sister always protects us, then we have confidence that connections provide safe haven. So one way to think about attachment styles is a way of understanding what happened during significant events in our lives. They capture a great deal about how we have adapted to circumstances around us, and reflect to what extent we have had to endure threats and trauma alone or with the aid of a connection to another person.

In *Building the Bonds of Attachment*, Daniel A. Hughes presents a succinct view of development attachment patterns. As viewed through a chronological lens, here is a summary of what happens in a child's first four years along with some additional insights about how that may affect the health of the child—and that person as an adult: [2]

- From birth to five months, a baby's main needs are food and safety. The infant falls into a biological rhythm with an attentive and responsive parent who brings a sense of calm and joy to interactions. Caregivers who don't deliver consistently, or perhaps seem resentful about having to feed and coddle the baby, or who may be emotionally absent from the interaction, plant the seeds of attachment problems for the child.

   An experiment involving primate mothers and newborns has direct implications for a human population and our understanding of how critical these first months of life are to long-term health. One group of mothers had ready access to food; they received it at the same place and time every day. A second group had to forage for their food. The third group got a combination of the two, but never knew how or when the provisions would arrive because it varied from one week to the next. The first group regularly attended to the food and safety needs of their children. The second group had some reduced maternal responsiveness. But the third group brought so much stress to their basic, biological interactions with their children that the babies experienced physiological damage.

The infants exhibited signs of stress, becoming fearful and/
or withdrawn. They also had changes in their spinal fluid
that correspond to changes linked to depression in humans.
The researchers followed the children into adolescence and
found that the third group continued to be more fearful and
withdrawn than the others.[3]

- The ability for attunement with others develops during the
first twelve months of life. Joyful play, mirroring gestures,
eye contact and other interactions stimulate a sense of
connection. Without that, a baby may become rigid and
withdrawn with other people and may avoid eye contact and
touch, or the child might become demanding, like the baby
in the "still face" experiment. She might scream and try to
grab the caregiver to get attention.

    Anita was a public health nurse in Washington, DC,
throughout her career. She was sent to a house out of concern
for a baby that another healthcare worker indicated was
listless, sickly, unresponsive and failing to thrive. After some
exposure to the home situation, Anita saw that the young
mother never talked to the baby and only touched him when
she had to do some motherly duty. The mother essentially
ignored the child. When the child was born, he seemed fine;
there was no good explanation for his deteriorated condition
other than the fact that he was spending his infancy alone
much of the time.

- From nine to eighteen months, attachment sequences
develop. As Hughes describes it, "Integration of autonomy
and attachment. Socialization with shame. Wide range of
socially meaningful feelings and behaviors are expressed
and organized. Much interest and joy. Much initiative while
accepting limits. Impulse control emerges."[4]

Caregivers at this developmental phase are generally helping the child experience key benchmarks, like learning to walk. The typical approach to something like that is to reduce the amount of physical assistance—from holding the child upright to holding his hand to letting him grab your pinky for reassurance—until the child develops autonomy. Ignoring the child so he figures out how to get up and walk on his own or overly supporting him so he becomes afraid of taking a step on his own are the types of experiences that take him away from feeling secure about himself and the people around him.

Shame is important in the context of society. We want children to learn to edit their behaviors, so shame is useful. Overdoing it has harmful ramifications, though, because shame is an isolating emotion. It puts a person in a corner alone, whereas other emotions tend to make you turn toward people and reach for them, whether they are "up" emotions like joy or "down" emotions like grief. A child who has experienced an inordinate amount of shame would likely have serious barriers to trust and self-esteem. Unfortunately, parents can cultivate secure attachments but a nanny or teacher may integrate shame as a tool to exact discipline.

- Cognitive capacity takes shape from eighteen to thirty-six months. This is when a child develops language, processing ideas internally by using words, as well as communicating with others in words.

  Signs that a child has attachment problems would be disorganized communication that's essentially nonsense and words that do nothing more than describe things rather than communicate wishes, feelings or intentions.

- In the period of thirty months to the four-year mark, the child develops cognitive differentiation. A sense of reciprocity takes shape, with the child starting to relate to other people with a greater range of emotions and ideas. Concepts such as "I," "you" and "we" have a growing sense of meaning.

Children who use words for things, not talking about how they feel or how anyone else feels, are distanced from a sense of reciprocity. Another red alert is the kind of randomness described above that makes their communication seem unfocused and/or out of control.[5]

From these brief descriptions we can easily see what the signs are of anxiously attached or avoidant children. But there is one more style that can come out of serious problems in early childhood: disorganized attachment. There is no clear, single type of attachment behavior for the disorganized individual. The child wants comfort from the caregiver, and sometimes finds it, but at the same time, feels fearful and insecure around the caregiver. He is confused and it shows.

The most extreme example of someone manifesting a disorganized attachment style would be a traumatized child who develops Dissociative Identity Disorder (DID), formerly known as Multiple Personality Disorder. Saroj Parida was an anxiously attached child. His young parents frequently left him alone with the houseboy when they went to parties. They loved him, but they often didn't have time for him. His older brother was gone most of the time, having been sent to school in another town. And then when Saroj was just about four years old, his attachment style got a jolt: The houseboy began sexually molesting Saroj and that triggered a serious mental illness, that is, DID. At least a dozen alternate personalities, or alters, emerged during the next forty years of Saroj's life. His attachment style could only be described as disorganized as the different personalities took prominence at different times.

Saroj's DID was not diagnosed until he was nearly fifty years old, after he'd built a successful career as a neonatologist. Three of his alters conspired to commit insurance fraud and, as a result of an FBI investigation, Saroj went to prison.

In an e-mail to Maryann, who became friends with Saroj and wrote about him extensively, he described the attachment styles of some of his alters:

> *Certainly Sissy [a five-year old] was anxiously attached.*
> *The 'infant' and the 'baby' were anxiously attached, too.*
> *The 'teenager' was also anxiously attached in a way. The*
> *avoidant ones would have been the angry ones ('Ravana'*
> *and 'Destroyer,' for example). The 'protector' cared for the*
> *core and the inner family. He got anxious when the angry*
> *ones emerged.*[6]

Saroj is still receiving therapy in prison and he has improved there, with episodes of dissociation happening far less frequently. Oddly enough, prison can become a safe and predictable environment, filled with people who chose carefully whom they will trust—people who are yearning for the co-regulation that comes from strong, positive connections. In prison, Saroj's ability to shape a secure attachment style is growing stronger. The following questionnaire will grade how your childhood affected your attachment style:

Family of Origin Attachment Questionnaire

When you were scared, sad or lonely as a child, your
   parents would:
   a) Hug you, soothe you and listen to your worries,
      fears and sadness, acknowledging your feelings and
      helping you identify what was wrong.
   b) Tell you "it's nothing," "don't worry," "It's not a big
      deal," "get over it" or "big boys don't cry."
   c) Become anxious and worried as well, amplifying
      your worries and fears, or get angry that you were
      emotional and tell you to stop feeling that way.

When you achieved something you worked hard on as a
child, your parents:
   a) Got excited, celebrated and made a fuss about your
      achievement, calling family members, friends, fully
      applauding your success.
   b) Didn't mention your accomplishment; life was too
      busy or overwhelming and they didn't have time to
      notice.
   c) Asked why you didn't do a little better; maybe you
      could have gotten an A+, not just an A. Or why you
      didn't win the championships even though you
      made it to the final round.

While you grew up with your siblings, your parents:
   a) Were equal in their praise/discipline/love with all
      siblings.
   b) Were too busy or tired to really engage with the kids
      equally, leaving you and your siblings to nurture
      one another.
   c) Maybe one parent in your house was the tyrant,
      yelling, criticizing and generally terrorizing
      everyone in the house.

When things felt unfair in your house, because one
   sibling got more stuff or maybe even the dog got more
   attention, you:
   a) Felt that one parent would see and notice that you
      were sad or felt left out or angry and try to talk to
      you about it.
   b) Felt that no one would care and it would be better to
      be quiet and not upset your parents.
   c) Would protest loudly, saying it was unfair and you
      were angry. With enough noise, someone would
      notice and take care of you.

When something went wrong at home or one of your
parents had a bad day, you were:
  a) Told that something was wrong and perhaps invited
     to be part of the solution.
  b) Never blamed for the problem, even though you
     might have caused it, because the problem was
     brushed aside.
  c) Blamed for the problem, if not wholly, then at least
     in part.

With this questionnaire, we are encouraging you to explore your
attachment style based on your family-of-origin interactions.

If you consistently answered A, your parents were careful to support your emotional needs. They made an effort to help you identify
what was happening for you emotionally in the moment, helping you
to learn to regulate your inner life. This skill set gives you the feeling
that you are emotionally secure; you can feel intense emotions and are
worthy of love. Your parents did a good job helping with your secure
attachment style and emotional resiliency.

If you answered most often with B, your caregiver was likely
emotionally shut down or avoidant. By their communicating to you
that your feelings were ridiculous or perhaps invalid, you were taught
to push your feelings away. You didn't learn to regulate your intense
feelings, and you may have developed a detached or overly anxious
attachment style to feel safe with your caregiver. Your caregiver probably did not feel safe dealing with his or her own intense emotions
and conveyed the same fear to you. As a result, you tend to deny, shut
down or avoid hurt, pain, disappointment and shame. As you push
your intense emotions down, the physical experience is of numbing
and distance from your moment-to-moment emotional connections.
In your adult relationships you are a withdrawer, that is, you tend
to shut down your emotions, dismissing your partner's emotional
experiences as well as your own. You devalue love, connection and
vulnerability.

It is possible, with an emotionally detached caregiver, that you may have developed an anxious, demanding style of emotional attachment, needing connection but not receiving it. Those of you who answered with C had a caregiver who was anxious and emotionally keyed up. By being too emotionally intense and personally disregulated, your caregiver gave you the sense that anxiety and fear are constants. You weren't taught to regulate your own emotions. Your attachment style may tend to be like that of a pursuer: you feel anxious that your partner can't be there for you, and even if he or she is, it is hard for you to trust that you are safe and attached. Your innermost fear is that you will be abandoned by your spouse or partner and that, deep down, you are not worthy of love.

Here is a heartbreaking example of how the issue of blame can play out. One of Trevor's childhood friends grew up in a family in which she got blamed for everything from tension between the parents to bankrupting the family. Her parents fell just short of accusing her of black magic when there was a power outage.

Probably the most damaging incident to her in terms of her sense of trust and safety involved her father, who had a business that was teetering on the brink of disaster and was seeking funding from a private source. That private source happened to be the father of a girl that Trevor's friend didn't get along with at school. When the friend's father did not get the funding, he blamed his daughter because of the contentious relationship she had with the other girl. His company went bankrupt and he said to his daughter, without any hesitation or remorse, "It's your fault."

Blame is a toxic element of any relationship, with blame and shame going hand in hand.

It involves a process of judgment that's massively human because it reflects a desire to keep each other in line for the sake of society, but it's also inhuman because it pushes people to the outskirts of that society.

The story of Trevor's friend's father illustrates vividly what blame is, that is, the process of shifting pain. In finding a scapegoat, we feel relieved of some intense experience like humiliation, sadness, anger or remorse. People in our culture tend to use blame heavy-handedly: All around us, we see politicians, celebrities, pundits, critics, religious leaders, teachers and other people of prominence in our lives and society rise up righteously and lay blame. With so much exposure to the exercise of blaming, it's difficult for the rest of us to resist jumping in and joining the party. But blaming is generally bad for the blamer as well as the person being beaten with the stick.

Blamers are set apart from other people, and above other people; they cannot be in an empathetic place with others. If you feel sick when someone representing your church, your government, your community or your family starts blaming someone for a "wrong-doing," it may be because you are hurt that the connection with that person feels broken—even if you aren't the one being blamed.

It's a double blow for the person who is being blamed. First, the person feels isolated due to the blame. The blamer minimizes his or her ability to co-regulate with members of the community. Second, the blamer elevates himself to a level of self-righteousness, so the person who receives the blame not only feels disconnection, but also "less than." Normal human reactions are either to be sad or angry.

When you incorporate blame into your intense relationships—either intentionally blaming and shaming or doing it reflexively because that's what you learned in your family of origin—it is like infusing your connection with a mental cancer.

DOES A TROUBLED CHILD BECOME A SICK ADULT?

We are not rigidly attached, but our attachment styles do have some consistency. Otherwise this approach to understanding human relationships and emotional processes would be less meaningful. The science of neuroplasticity (or brain plasticity) confirms that we can rewire our neural pathways and synapses as a result of changes in our environment and behavior, as well as from injury or trauma. Even so, it's not likely that our attachment styles would change overnight.

Many times, couples in EFT therapy start to move through and past their troubles as soon as they surrender into the relationship. They abandon the externals that have seemed to define their relationship—for example, power struggles, blaming and fighting—and explore their connection with no agenda other than they wanted to know how it felt to truly trust each other. When you're wrapped up in ego and trying to outperform other people moment after moment, you miss opportunities to experience the deeply satisfying aspects of connection.

Maryann and her partner, Jim, were on vacation in Costa Rica a few years ago. One evening they were having dinner with friends at an outdoor café and Maryann suddenly felt as though her body was one with the environment; it seemed as though she didn't know where her physical self ended, because the temperature and humidity seemed to match those of her body so perfectly. She asked the other people at the table if they felt the same way and they did. It was a kind of shared ethereal experience. This physical sensation conveys the sense of what we mean when we say that couples surrender into their relationship and connect as though nothing separates them. It is a completely secure and relaxing sensation.

Someone with a lone-cowboy mentality might dismiss this or criticize this feeling: "You've lost yourself!" It's actually quite the opposite: You've found more of yourself.

The experience of feeling "one with the universe" or one with another person suggests an almost meditative state that is definitely something to strive for in terms of physical and mental health. Meditation is a powerful practice supporting healing and well-being. It can be an individual pursuit or it can also be practiced in pairs or groups.

There are different forms of meditation, which one might describe as consciousness without thought. Others would be consciousness with a single focus, as on breathing, or focus on a single theme. The latter type would describe meditation in the Roman Catholic tradition, in which a group might spend time silently contemplating the suffering of Jesus Christ, for example. It could also involve two people concurrently focusing on their relationship as a well of peace.

A Stanford University psychologist named Philippe Goldin compiled findings from a variety of studies related to mindful meditation and summarized some compelling results. Positive effects on health and healing were associated with a wide range of conditions, both mental and physical. These included cancer, depression, smoking, fibromyalgia, chronic pain, skin disorders and binge eating.

At the heart of such benefits was the effect of meditation on stress. It's like cool water on hot coals. The research analysis discusses meditation as both a religious practice and a medical practice and, even though it refers to meditation as an "autogenic therapy"—"auto" meaning self—that should not be interpreted as implying that the person was alone while meditating. "Autogenic" means that the effect was produced within the body as a result of what the person did, not that the person was necessarily alone when he or she did it. The analysis notes:

> *The utilization of self-regulatory capacity is one of the purposes of autogenic therapy, a method consisting of exercises focused on the limbs, lungs, heart, diaphragm and head. The physiological response is muscle relaxation, increased peripheral blood flow, lower heart rate and blood pressure, slower and deeper breathing, and reduced oxygen consumption. Autogenic training is applicable in most pathological conditions associated with stress, and can be used preventively or as a complement to conventional treatment.*[7]

Richard Davidson, neuroscientist at the University of Wisconsin, conducted a major study of meditation practitioners by wiring their skulls with sensors. The effort was part of his ongoing work at the forefront of neuroplasticity research. Not only did he find that meditation "changes your brain and therefore changes what you are,"[8] but he also found the world's happiest man. Tests confirmed that when he is meditating on compassion, French monk Matthieu Ricard produces unprecedented levels of gamma waves, which are associated with consciousness, attention, learning and memory. This is all left prefrontal cortex activity that, theoretically anyway, gives Ricard an enormous ability to feel happiness and avert negativity.

As for the sensation of being one with the universe, it reflects a shutdown of the orientation associational area of the brain, that is, the area above the right ear called the right parietal region. People in a state of deep meditation perceive that boundaries don't exist between them and their environment. Andrew Newburg, a radiologist at the University of Pennsylvania Hospital, documented the phenomenon in brain-imaging studies involving monks and nuns in states they themselves called either meditation or prayer.[9]

Citing the benefits to health and well-being of his neuroplasticity research focused on meditation, Davidson noted:

> *We have been looking for [twelve] years at the effect of*
> *short and long-term mind training through meditation*
> *on attention, on compassion, on emotional balance. We've*
> *found remarkable results with long-term practitioners*
> *who did 50,000 rounds of meditation, but also with three*
> *weeks of [twenty] minutes a day, which of course is more*
> *applicable to our modern times.*[10]

When EFT therapists like Trevor guide couples to a state of surrendering to their relationships, to feeling the connection between them as people who have experienced love together, they are essentially guiding them down the path to a meditative type of state. The aim is to move from a fear that the "me" will be swallowed by the "we," and into the stress-free experience of feeling trusting and vulnerable as part of a "we." (Trevor notes an important caveat here: Not all couples belong together; that's just a fact of life. Sometimes this therapeutic approach is not what two individuals need; sometimes it is true that one person has no basis for trusting the other and could be damaged emotionally and/or even physically by making the emotional boundaries between them porous.)

Some psychotherapists would refer to this me-we work that Trevor does with couples as an exercise in "self-differentiation," a term coined by Murray Bowen, who greatly influenced the nature of couples and family therapy. Self-differentiation describes the interplay between autonomy, or separateness, of the individual and connection, or togetherness, with another person. That sounds good, but the process of developing self-differentiation focuses a great deal on personal power and on the articulation of personal needs.[11]

On this matter, Trevor parts company with colleagues in describing the me-we process she uses with couples as one of self-differentiation, which intellectualizes relationships too much. Trevor's work is about self-awareness in the context of the people and relationships in your life. With that in mind, self-actualization cannot happen without a connection to another. That's a very different, heart-based model.

In this model, attachment styles become a path for us to understand cycles of distress for ourselves and our partners. They also serve as a path to repairing the emotional issues that were an integral part of our childhood. So the answer to the question posed at the beginning of this section, "Does a Troubled Child Become a Sick Adult?" is, "No. A troubled child—that is, one with serious attachment issues—does not have to become a sick adult." However, it's important to note that a troubled child needs powerful emotional stimuli to move toward a secure attachment style.

Many people pass on their attachment behaviors to their children, unaware that their parenting reflects some of the pain their own parents infused in their lives. For example, Carole, one mother we know, received love and attention from her mother only when she was sick. Other than that, she got a version of the "still face" described in chapter 1. A neurological grooving occurs when an important emotional event like this recurs. It not only affected her parenting, but will possibly affect her daughter's parenting as well. The mom would spoil the daughter so thoroughly when she got sick that, eventually, the child wanted a sick day periodically because she enjoyed the extra attention and sense of feeling loved and valued. Mom and daughter would wear matching pajamas on the child's "mental health days" away from school. Carole has been programmed to carry that sense of "sickness is good for relationships" forward in her own family life.

Parents can also shape attachment behaviors by suppressing a child's impulses to act one way or another. They might respond negatively or maybe just neutrally, so the child gets the message, "Don't do that."

Parents expect children to behave in a certain way, so it's only natural that children have to hold back or change the way they express themselves sometimes. We all have to suppress some aspects of ourselves in our parents' home. A result of that is that we find a way to let that part of ourselves out when we're adults.

A friend of Maryann's who is a prolific author always does launch parties for her books. When her husband asked her why she "wasted money" on these events, she explained that she needed the celebration. Growing up, even though she excelled at academics and sports, her parents never really made a fuss over her. It was as though they expected her to do well because she had a lot of natural gifts. She's a very secure person, aware that the need to celebrate is part of her emotional process. Making up for having suppressed a part of oneself as a child does not always surface in a happy or healthy way.

A good example of this is seen in Mike and Diane's marriage. Within the first year, he had an affair. Ten years and two children later, she decided to have a retaliatory affair. He is very anxiously attached; she is avoidant. The rancor in their relationship had escalated to the point where they couldn't converse, so they sought counseling.

During their first eighteen months of couple's therapy, the relationship seemed to improve. Then, during one session, it was as though someone had set off a stink bomb in the room. Diane began talking about a friend of hers who had behaved in a mean way. Leveraging a connection her husband had, she had arranged to get the friend a substantial discount on extensive home improvements—for which the husband's friend was never paid.

Mike was aghast that Diane would ever consider the person a friend after the woman had financially wounded his colleague. He wanted her to choose between the two of them, not actually spitting out an ultimatum, but asking her to decide to side with him and leave the bad friend behind.

"There are two sides to every story," she protested weakly. He wouldn't budge and the conversation took on an accusatory tone. And based on how both of them described the situation, the bad friend seemed to have the patina of a chronic user.

These exchanges about the friend occurred during a single therapy session.

Mike verged on furious. He didn't calm down and try to work through the path established as part of the session until he heard more of the story. There were other female friends in Diane's life who seemed to show exploitive, and even abusive, behavior as well. She made excuses for all of them and seemed ready to rationalize their actions no matter how distasteful or hurtful they were.

And then Diane listened to the story of the scorpion and the frog crossing the river. The scorpion is catching a ride across the river and stings the frog on his head. As the frog is dying, he asks the scorpion, "Why did you do that to me?" The scorpion replies, "I'm a scorpion, dummy."

Diane came to the realization that she would plunge into denial about the part of her so-called friends that would eventually hurt her. But why?

Diane could only be described as extremely beautiful physically, but she grew up in a home with an older sister who rated the term "homely." Diane's mother catered to the older sister, just assuming that Diane would always be fine; she would always get the boys and the opportunities because she was so pretty. If this is beginning to sound like Cinderella to you, that's how it sounded to us. The only things lacking were the pumpkin carriage, Prince Charming and a glass slipper.

The older sister took scissors to Diane's favorite outfits, bullied her incessantly and lied about Diane's responses. The mother always sided with the big sister.

As a result of this upbringing, Diane developed an extremely avoidant attachment style. She had to suppress the feelings of "I'm not safe in my own house" and "Nobody will stand up for me." To save her life—perhaps literally—she had to deny her feelings that people were out to get her.

Mike understood: His wife didn't even recognize when someone was being cruel or mean to her because she spent much of her life having to shove that aside into a mental closet. She grew up with no one sticking up for her. Mean treatment was the status quo.

His anger disappeared. The transition from "How could you not stand up to me?" to "Now I understand why you process pain this way" was *immediate*. Mike and Diane left that session holding hands and with a profound sense of love vibrating between them.

We invite you to dig into your own childhood and make a list of needs and tendencies you suppressed within your family. Here are some questions to guide you.

Keep this thought in mind as you start: It is hard for many of us to look critically or objectively at our childhoods. Most of us had pretty good childhoods. Our parents were around and we got mostly what we needed. Yet, even in the best of situations, our parents couldn't possibly be there for us all the time. And some of us grew up in negative atmospheres.

Take some time to think about when your parents couldn't be there.

What happened for you?
Who was there for you?
If you questioned your parents for not being there, were they willing to talk, take responsibility and do better or did they shut you down?

Did you feel that your parents found joy in your very being?

Did you feel as though you were a burden?

Did your parents criticize you or shame you when you didn't meet their expectations?

Who praised you?

Did one or both of your parents promise things and events but not follow through?

Were they open and accepting of your special foibles and personality quirks?

If so, how did they show it?

What about your personality/person did your parents dislike and try to suppress?

Where you ever afraid in your house?

Did your parents value your opinions, hopes and aspirations?

Did they squash your dreams?

Once you delve into the deeper aspects of what went well and what didn't go so well in your childhood, it is important to draw some parallels with your adult relationships. We all develop our map of love based on what we learned in our families of origin. If you experienced connection or "love" in a household where your parents were angry and critical, it is highly likely that you will find a partner who creates the same process in your adult relationship.

The love map we develop is based on our attachments and if we felt unloved, undervalued and minimized in our family, we most likely will find a partner who makes us feel exactly the same way. That is our comfort level, being attracted to and connecting with a familiar experience, even if it's negative.

Next, consider how those aspects of your childhood inform your adult relationship.

Do you feel that your partner delights in your very being?

Does your partner make promises and not keep them?

Does your partner listen to you and attune to you or do you feel
he/she doesn't have the time or attention for you?

Is your partner supportive of your hopes and dreams? Or does
he or she scoff at them and minimize your aspirations?

Does your partner criticize or shame you?

Do you feel as if you can be fully yourself with your partner?

Do you feel that your partner accepts all your foibles and quirks?

Or does it feel like your partner is trying to change you?

Is your partner willing to hear you out when you feel he/she is not
available, not connected or does something hurtful to you?

Or does your partner shut you down when you ask for change?

Does your partner tend to blame you when things go wrong?

If so, does it remind you of your childhood?

How do you feel and react when you get blamed for something?

Was it okay to be wrong in your family?

When strong emotions come up, what do you do with them?

The point is that your family of origin does shape who you are, but you
can also forge relationships along the way that dramatically change
your attachment behaviors. That dramatic change can help you heal
emotionally, psychologically and even physically; the opposite can
happen as well. And then, there is the person who maintains the status
quo from childhood through adulthood.

As part of her work developing Emotionally-Focused Therapy
(EFT), Susan Johnson pinpointed two questions that adults in intense
relationships think about, if not also verbalize. The answers are at the
heart of an emotional healing process. The first is, "Are you there for
me?" meaning, "Do you have my back?" and "Can I trust you?" And
the second is, "Am I important to you?" Going to your partner's once-
a-year piano recital, instead of playing golf (again) on a Saturday afternoon, is a way of saying "yes" to that question. When both questions
are answered in the affirmative through words and actions, then even
a couple with lots of attachment baggage can start to bring their hearts
together.

Another aspect of healing has more to do with being than it does with words or specific actions. A partner with an anxious attachment style is a pursuer, constantly trying to find solutions to things. It can drive the other person crazy because he or she may not feel he or she is doing enough or doing things well enough. Moving to a state of receiving affection, being receptive in an emotional way, is a vital part of infusing the relationship with health.

DETERMINING YOUR ADULT ATTACHMENT STYLE

We have created an informal questionnaire to help you ascertain some things about your attachment style. It's not a test instrument like the Attachment Interview Protocol that a researcher might use. This is just a simple set of questions to help you determine what informs how you behave and react to your partner as well as others in your life. Keep in mind that behaviors are reciprocal, so this set of questions may lead you to an understanding of why your partner and others respond to you in a particular way, too.

Couples Attachment Questionnaire

When your partner is annoyed, frustrated or even angry with you, you:
   a) Don't react to the anger, but ask what is going on with your partner and offer to help by empathizing with his/her situation.
   b) Become afraid to make matters worse, thinking that whatever you say will only make your partner angrier; you pull back. Perhaps you don't know what to do, so you shut down.
   c) Become angry and fight back.

When you feel as if your partner is distant and not interested in your feelings or what you need, you:

a) Ask your partner for attention and understanding, saying you feel lonely and disconnected from him or her.
b) Clam up and say less, hoping your partner will pull it out of you, because he or she really *should* know you well enough to read your mind.
c) Yell loudly and criticize your partner to get attention.

When you disagree, who yells the loudest or says the most?
a) You're a listener, not a yeller.
b) If your partner starts yelling, you leave the room—or maybe the house.
c) You do.

Who is the first to "make nice" or attempt a repair after you have a fight?
a) You are.
b) Your partner is.
c) Both are: sometimes you, sometimes your partner.

When you observe your partner talking to another person at a party who is attractive, you:
a) Wait until your partner's conversation is over and later tell your partner that it was hard for you to watch him or her talking to an attractive person. It made you feel worried and vulnerable. Then you ask for reassurance and reconnection from your partner.
b) Walk away and ask for a glass of wine, vowing never to talk about it but secretly hoping your partner sees how hurt you are.
c) Get angry, interrupt the conversation and criticize your partner there or later, blaming your partner for being insensitive or rude.

When your partner is feeling an intense emotion (fear, joy, grief) you:
    a) Reach out, empathizing with your partner, allowing your partner to feel the intensity of the emotion while staying with him or her in the experience, hoping to provide comfort and support.
    b) Try to help him or her by saying "this is not a big deal," "it will go away" or "don't pay attention to it."
    c) Try to step in and solve the problem in order to alleviate the emotion.

When something goes wrong, you:
    a) Aim for shared understanding of what happened.
    b) Either take the blame or go straight to blame-sharing to avoid confrontation.
    c) Blame the other person.

If you chose the first answer to most of the questions you are most likely a securely attached person. This means you are comfortable with your own emotions and able to express them to your partner. You also are able to empathize and be available for your partner when he or she is feeling strong emotions instead of feeling attacked or defensive.

Being securely attached leads to positive interpersonal behaviors. A securely attached person tends to be a good listener, able to reserve judgment, and feels that he or she can be trusted and trust in return. Securely attached relationships are loving, stable, attuned and empathetic.

If you tended to pick the second answer you are probably more avoidantly attached. You tend to dismiss your own emotions. When asked how you feel about things, you might respond, "I don't know." When stressed or emotional about something, you withdraw and perhaps watch television or read a book, but you do not acknowledge the feelings underlying the withdrawal. When your partner is upset, you freeze up or leave, shutting down emotionally. When you feel overwhelmed, you can't empathize with the pain your partner is feeling.

What happens to you in relationships is that you tend to quell your emotions and stay at arm's length from your feelings and others. As a result, you tend to come across as less than empathetic, maybe cold and unfeeling. Your partner may feel emotionally abandoned by you, causing him or her to come after you to blame or criticize you, hoping to get some kind of emotional connection.

As an avoidantly attached person, you are fearful of rejection. You withdraw from intense emotional displays from your partner as a way to survive (a sympathetic nervous system response). You get flooded by your partner's intensity and shut down, causing your partner to feel emotionally abandoned.

Behavior patterns between two avoidantly-attached people are like roommates living together; two polite, detached and lonely people.

An avoidant person and an anxiously attached person result in negative cyclical behaviors known as pursue-withdraw. (This becomes clearer after the explanation that follows of an anxious attachment style.) This is the most common couple connection and most couples have some aspect of pursue-withdraw in their behavior patterns.

If you picked the third answer more often in the last questionnaire, you may be an anxiously attached person. As an anxiously attached person, you are on guard for your partner's emotional abandonment. You can't trust that your partner is really there for you. This means that even when your partner is doing loving things and looking for connection, you may not be able to take it in.

An anxious partner is often called controlling or jealous, because he or she believes the way to calm down and feel safe is to know where his or her partner is all of the time. Control is not connection (which is empathetic, safe attunement); it is about the pursuer trying to feel safe and attempting to calm his or her sympathetic nervous system.

If you are an anxious pursuer, you respond to a threat by fighting, not freezing or fleeing. You might use a loud voice, criticism and blame to try to get attention from your withdrawing partner. However, your behavior patterns tend to push your withdrawer/avoidant partner even farther away, accomplishing the very opposite of what you yearn for: connection.

Two anxious pursuers rarely end up together, because the relationship would be incendiary. They couldn't calm one another down and the relationship would eventually blow up.

There is no judgment associated with your answers. It's not a terrible thing to admit to being anxiously attached or avoidant; neither one makes you "bad" at relationships. In addition, even securely attached people typically have some issues that a therapist might label "unresolved." So you may feel as though there are glitches in your responses—that you aren't "all" secure, for example. Bob and Angie, one couple we know, are two securely attached people who periodically have fights related to either his or her competence. It turns out that both of them felt they had to work extra hard as children to get their parents to admit they were good at something. As they grew up, Bob and Angie carried sensitivity about being appreciated and recognized for their competence. Keep those kinds of exceptions in mind and use our last questionnaire to better understand yourself and your partner.

PART III

Your Relationships

CHAPTER 6

Who (and What) Is in Your Heart?

The heart is a vital organ that tells us a lot about our state of emotion. It is also a symbol of emotion that tells us a lot about our physical state. For that reason, "heart disease" can refer to both an ailing body part and emotional trauma.

First, let's discuss who is in your heart, also known as people with whom you share the closeness we might call love. We will also look at how love feels and functions and how it is detectable by hard science. After that, we will focus on the impact of those love relationships on your heart, the organ. People feel both positive and negative effects of relationships throughout the body but a good place to start focusing on some specific effects is the heart.

LOVE AS A FELT SENSE

When Trevor asks clients to locate a certain feeling in their bodies, they typically look at her with skepticism. Their first reaction is usually "Are you serious?" Some say, "In my heart," if the feeling is lost love. For most feelings, however, the idea of making a visceral connection to an emotion is completely foreign to many people.

Most of us don't acknowledge or honor that all our emotions are first felt physically. When we are afraid, we feel it by our hearts beating faster and our breaths getting shallower. All emotions—sadness, happiness, shame, disgust—are first registered in our bodies. As an EFT therapist, Trevor's job is often to guide clients through the "felt sense" of events.

If a physician asked you, "Where does it hurt?" or "Where does it itch?" you could probably give an answer without hesitation. In putting the concept of "felt sense" to work in your life, you will be making the same kind of link between emotion and your body—and you will give yourself and your loved one(s) a powerful tool to support health and healing.

For example, Trevor might ask a husband, "When your wife tells you she appreciates what you do for her, where do you feel it?" He might respond, "I feel it in my shoulders, maybe more relaxed." He describes how he feels more at ease or safer within the relationship at that moment. That is his "felt sense" of her regard for him. Let's say that recognition of felt sense started happening on a regular basis—for both of them. He's tremendously stressed out from something that happens at the office. She sees that his shoulders are raised and maybe his arms are drawn in tightly to his body. She tells him how grateful she and the kids are for what he does, especially knowing what he has to put up with sometimes. Shoulders down, he immediately starts to de-stress.

Creating change moments or enactments like this in the therapy room is the rewiring process of couples coming to greater connection and relatedness. Being able to identify the experience of love and regard for one another is an important part of healing and reconnecting. It is the emotional underpinning of "re-coupling," literally the opposite of telling a couple to have a 5:1 ratio of communication. (That's an old-school approach to getting a couple to make nice: being sure to say something positive before you voice a negative. Not bad advice, but it doesn't dig into the deeper issues.)

In the context of an intimate relationship, love as a felt sense involves the other person's body and mind as much as it involves yours. A loving couple doesn't feel love *for* each other; they feel love *in* each other. Love, therefore, is the felt sense that you exist in the heart, mind and soul of another person. It is not a lofty concept but a humble one.

Consider how the concept of synchronicity is central to understanding/feeling this
definition of love. This is about a patterned,
rhythmic connection with another person—
someone with whom we have laid down positive neurological pathways in our brain. It
might be symbolized like this:

The difficulty some people have in
grasping this definition is that sources typically define it intellectually
as an outgoing emotion—one that a person experiences and projects.
According to the Merriam-Webster dictionary, love is:

(1) : strong affection for another arising out of kinship or
personal ties <maternal love for a child>
(2) : attraction based on sexual desire : affection and tenderness
felt by lovers
(3) : affection based on admiration, benevolence, or common
interests <love for his old schoolmates>[1]

In contrast to those "push" definitions of love, our definition
focuses on the incoming nature of love. It is the experience of your
existence in another person's mind and heart.

Felt Sense Exercise

Think of the last time your partner or the person closest to
you did something kind and caring for you. Feel where it
rests in your body as you recall it.

- Does your heart feel bigger?
- Can you breathe deeper?
- Is there less stress in your shoulders?
- Anything else?

Try to feel a positive experience in your body and think about that for a few moments. Expand on it. When we have the "felt sense" that we are safe, that we are loved, valued and known, we have less tension in our bodies. We can actually feel the experience in our physical beings.

Now think of a time that you were under attack. Maybe your partner criticized you for doing something hurtful or selfish. Where did you experience that in your body? Really try to locate the physicality of the moment.

- Did your stomach churn?
- Did you feel like your breathing was restricted?
- Did you tense up your shoulders or your fists?
- Anything else?

Making contact with the bodily experience of emotion is vitally important to understanding your emotions—and to having those emotions be the "shift in integration" that we described in chapter 2. The more aware of your own physical process you can become, the more you can share it with your partner. The more your partner grasps the connection for you, the better he or she is able to help you thrive and heal.

An essential element of love as a felt sense is vulnerability. An October 2012 issue of *USA Weekend* cited Brené Brown's book, *Daring Greatly: How the Courage to Be Vulnerable Transforms the Way We Live, Love, Parent, and Lead*, in an article called "Hidden secret to success: vulnerability." The article asserted: "Strength and overconfidence are often celebrated as traits for getting ahead, but vulnerability may play an equally important role…" in part because it evokes change, is ubiquitous and reduces regret.[2]

So what's love got to do with it?

Regarding change, Brown describes vulnerability as a state of being "all in," which she explains is a complete, high-risk commitment.[3] Everything could go wrong; everything could go right, too. To move to a vulnerable state requires a great deal of change for most people. This is especially relevant for people in a culture such as ours in America where we grab for figurative body armor at the slightest threat to our emotions. Throughout time, poets and lyricists have described vulnerability—an unprotected openness—as a key to true love. One of Maryann's favorite quotes about it comes from the contemporary Japanese author Haruki Murakami, who said, "What happens when people open their hearts?"..."They get better."[4] Consider how much you might have to change just to embrace that sentiment as truth.

Brown's second point, that vulnerability is everywhere, reminds us that everyone—from CEOs of Fortune 100 companies to a child who is hungry and alone on a city street—has moments of feeling vulnerable. Even rich, powerful executives know that things might go terribly wrong, personally or professionally, and that is scary. They are vulnerable and they need to accept that as part of their humanity. Ultimately, when they come face to face with that part of themselves, they find the strength to be vulnerable through their relationships. They don't walk out of a session thinking that an uptick in the Dow Jones Industrial Average will give them the long-term ability to cope with media scrutiny, for example. They see their personal strength as coming from the spouse, children and friends who respect them and will stand by them "no matter what." Those people who love them give them permission to be less than perfect—and that's a key part of feeling vulnerable.

The third of Brown's points is that vulnerability helps reduce regret. This is probably one reason why more and more people are making bucket lists. Some of the most enticing things on a bucket list are scary, and yet these are the experiences that people desire when they think they have nothing else to lose. Brown is suggesting, "Why wait?" The odd relationship that Jack Nicholson as the terminally ill corporate executive and Morgan Freeman as the blue-collar mechanic formed in the movie *The Bucket List* was all about the role of vulnerability in love—how it contributes to healing and joy.

PROOF OF LOVE IN THE BRAIN

Arthur Aron, who is on the faculty at Stony Brook University and Associate Editor for the *Journal of Personality and Social Psychology*, focuses much of his research on identifying interpersonal closeness as cognitive overlap between self and other. He looks at how the brains of people in love are somehow linked. As a corollary, he has done studies examining how relationship experiences are mapped in the brain.

In a 2010 study he did with Stony Brook University colleague Bianca Acevedo, the two used Functional Magnetic Resonance Imaging (fMRI) to try to detect the signs of romantic love in the brains of men and women who asserted they still had intense feelings for their spouses after an average of 21 years of marriage.[5] The result was "Neural correlates of long-term intense romantic love," published in *Social Cognitive and Affective Neuroscience*. It's the first bit of research to image and analyze which regions of the brain activate when a person feels deeply in love.[6]

The really intriguing fact they discovered is that the brains of these long-time lovers had the same kind of activity as couples who had just recently fallen in love. In both cases, the regions of the brain that had fireworks were the reward and motivation regions which are rich in dopamine.[7]

Aron is no longer alone—or one of only a few researchers—using imaging to study love. Daniel J. Siegel and Allan N. Schore, who are colleagues at the University of California, have also explored what love looks like in the brain. Their term for the field of study is interpersonal neurobiology and it's premised on the fact that our relationships, from birth to death, alter our brain circuits related to memory and emotion.[8]

Siegel and Schore, among others, have observed that brain scans of baby and mother reveal that the two are linked, synchronous beings. These early experiences lay down a neural pattern for the baby's attachment style and behaviors. By no means is this the end of the story, though. Their brain imaging studies also document that subsequent relationships affect that circuitry:

"...as a wealth of imaging studies highlight, the neural alchemy continues throughout life as we mature and forge friendships, dabble in affairs, succumb to romantic love, choose a soul mate. The body remembers how that oneness with Mother felt, and longs for its adult equivalent."[9]

The most powerful finding of the imaging studies is that loving relationships alter the brain the most.

LOVE REDUCES DEMANDS ON THE BODY

As a survival mechanism, as much time passes, organisms have to consume more energy than they expend if they intend to reproduce. Since humans use substantial energy to analyze, evaluate, create, judge, problem solve and make decisions, it makes sense that reducing that energy contributes to our survivability.

James Coan researched how relationships play into that goal. One result is his Social Baseline Model, which proposes that people are hard-wired to maintain close proximity to other humans as part of a strategy to reduce energy expenditure relative to energy consumption.[10] That means that when we have to go it alone, the energy cost of interacting with our environment escalates. Without people around to help—not only by providing tangible assistance, but simply by being near us—there is no perception of risk sharing or load distribution.

Coan cites his experiment with a backpack as illustrating this effect. It involves putting a heavy backpack on a person who is alone and having him stand facing a hill. When asked how steep the hill is, he might give an answer like "forty-five degrees." For the next part of the experiment, another person is brought in to stand beside him; the scenario is that they would climb the hill together. Suddenly, the hill appears to be more like a thirty-degree incline, or maybe a twenty-degree incline. The point is that the hill appears steeper than it really is when the person is alone, so he requires more motivation to climb it. The brain of the lone person tries to "talk" him out of hiking up the hill.

Coan said, "Our brain is always messing with our perception. The brain plays tricks on us to motivate our behavior."[11]

Our brains are particularly sensitive to the load-sharing significance of our loving connections. People in trusted relationships will invest less effort in their negative impulses, leaving them less reactive to threat cues and other signs of possible harm. So, we are wired to outsource some of the things that occupy our minds to those with whom we have close relationships. A practical result is that our brains use less energy.

This load-sharing strategy, especially in adult attachment relationships, probably develops as the brains of the people in a relationship become conditioned to one another, especially in the context of coping with threats. Coan said, "Over time, individuals in attachment relationships literally become part of each other's emotion regulation strategy. This is not metaphorical, but literal, even at the neural level."[12] For example, someone who has been alone for a long time may have learned to exercise his prefrontal cortex to try and regulate his threat responses. The prefrontal cortex is that part of the brain that is active in analyzing and decision-making. Coan's Social Baseline Model predicts that when that person establishes an attachment relationship, his perception of the degree to which his environment is threatening or dangerous will change; he'll start using his prefrontal cortex a lot less.[13] It's a natural shift because his brain assumes a decrease in the need for regulating emotion. After he feels secure in the relationship, the level of interdependence the two people have as it pertains to regulating emotions can become very strong. A sad reminder of this occurs when one partner suddenly dies or leaves. The other partner is truly at a loss for coping with some of the most basic stresses coming at him in his environment.

A study of National Basketball Association (NBA) teams found essentially the same thing that Coan did in his work, but instead of seeing the effect of a "pat on the backpack," the researchers focused on fist bumps, high fives, chest bumps, leaping shoulder bumps, chest punches, head slaps, head grabs, low fives, high tens, full hugs, half hugs and team huddles. An effort by a University of California, Berkeley team, "Tactile Communication, Cooperation, and Performance," concluded that NBA teams that touched each other often early in the season performed better than their competition later in the season. Touch signals cooperation and promotes trust. It gives the players a sense of distributing risk and load sharing, as Coan discussed in his description of the Social Baseline Model. And so, even though the members of the other teams were just as big and just as fast, they were actually working harder to score than the members of the team that had an enhanced sense of spreading the work around.[14]

Robert Sutton, a Stanford University professor and organizational psychologist, has written a great deal about the power of nonsexual touching; he covered the NBA study for *Psychology Today*. In his article, he highlighted the value of the study in terms of all kinds of relationships, not just those on the basketball court. Trust is our most highly developed sense at birth, and it is a distinctly human way of quickly communicating significant emotions like gratitude, sympathy and love.[15] In a second, a touch can convey, *I'm here for you*, a sentiment that instantly sends the signal to the recipient's brain, *My life just got easier.*

WHAT AFFECTS *YOUR* HEART MORE—LOVE OR STRESS?

A positive emotional component of our lives is essential for clear and complete thinking, as well as health. Human beings have a reduced ability to think when under certain kinds of stress. We down-regulate in a good relationship, meaning that the stress levels drop. If you are compromised in your personal relationships, you are less capable of robust thought and, therefore, have a diminished ability to make lifestyle choices that benefit your health.

Lifestyle/Relationship Questionnaire

Throughout our day we are affected continuously by our relationships and they make us feel differently moment by moment. In order to understand what is happening, you need to track your felt sense of your day and your interactions. This is a first pass at being present with your feelings and observing your relationships and behaviors.

Section 1

Let's start at the beginning of the day and go through the day with a focus on your feelings and reactions. Select the one answer that fits best, or applies most often:

When you wake up, what is your general feeling?
  a) Tired and cranky, maybe even angry to have to wake up and pissed off with the world
  b) Anxious because of little sleep and negative dreams
  c) Rejuvenated by a good night's sleep

What is the feeling of your first interaction of the day, generally?
  a) A negative or angry exchange
  b) Disconnected, lonely; little exchange with spouse/partner/kids or others
  c) Happy, loving, gentle interaction with partner, kids, pets

How do you feel about getting dressed? Eating breakfast? Getting out the door?
  a) Stressed, angry, frustrated
  b) Disconnected, not engaged, going through the motions
  c) Happy to be up and moving

When you get to work/school, what goes on for you?
  a) Angry that no one seems to care that you are there

b) No feeling, no connection and a sense of distance

c) Happy to be there, welcomed, warm feeling

When you are finished with work/school do you engage in a hobby? Work out? Perhaps sing in a church group such as a choir?

a) Hostile to the whole idea of activities and socializing, you go home and are alone

b) Hard to drag yourself to the activity; you are involved with something you don't care about

c) It feels good to sing in the choir or do community service

On the weekends, do you:

a) Do something alone, like shop or clean the house, because you just don't enjoy being around others all that much

b) Feel left out of social events, wishing to be more connected

c) Do an activity you love with people you like and know

Did you have any pain today? What hurts? Did you:

a) Tell everyone around you

b) Suffer in silence but use body language to convey your desire for attention

c) Tell a friend/partner/child

Of the following people in your life, who do you think of most?

a) Parent

b) Spouse/Partner

c) Boyfriend/Girlfriend

d) Children

e) Grandparent

f) Friend

What are the feelings that come to you when you think of that person?
  a) Anger, betrayal, perhaps disappointment; not knowing if you feel safe with that person in an emotional and/or physical sense
  b) Disconnect, nothing, disengagement
  c) Warmth, love, connection, safety, belonging

What do you do with your feelings about this person you think of often?
  a) Get angry if that person isn't understanding and available to speak with, yelling, criticizing and possibly blaming the person for your bad feelings
  b) Block your feelings; it is too uncomfortable to talk about feelings and your partner probably wouldn't listen anyway or might make fun of you
  c) Talk to that person about your feelings—good, bad or otherwise—because he or she is open to hearing about your feelings and supports you (This makes you feel better, getting things off your chest.)

When your partner/spouse is showing you kindness/love, do you:
  a) Push it away, thinking this is a little strange or uncomfortable
  b) Not even know; you are not in tune with loving moments so you can't feel them or recognize them
  c) Welcome connection and feel the love from your spouse in you

Section 2

Give a "yes" or "no" answer, depending on what is true for you most often:

Do you feel valued by your spouse/partner?

Do you feel that your spouse/partner understands you and cherishes you?

Do you feel that you can share all aspects of yourself with your partner? Your aspirations, dreams and hopes? Your fantasies?

Do you feel that if you asked your partner to accompany you to the opera (something he or she would despise), would he or she still go because of love for you?

Does your partner make you feel like you are his/her priority in life? Do you express your gratitude and your appreciation for your partner?

Section 3

Now, the focus will be more on habits and behaviors. Whereas the last two sections clearly involve answers that are preferable in terms of indicating your happiness and satisfaction in relationships, not all of these answers are weighted in the same way.

Do you have your phone with you during meals with your partner? With your kids? With your friends?

Did you have a midmorning snack? Did you feel like you really needed that snack or did you find the act of eating comforting, or perhaps distracting from something you didn't want to do?

Did you have a mid-afternoon snack?

Did you have an evening snack?

Did you laugh today? Did you feel happy? Were you:

    a) Alone?

    b) With a partner/friend, or someone else close to you?

    c) In a group of colleagues or acquaintances?

    d) With a group of strangers?

What was the best thing that happened to you today?
What was the worst thing that happened to you today?
Is there anything you did today that you regret or feel
   guilty about?
Is there anything you neglected to do that you feel bad
   about?

INTERPRETING THE QUESTIONNAIRE

Taking some time to get a sense of how often and how well
you connect to those around you is important. Science is
proving to us that our bodies and immune systems are
stronger when we are in safe and emotionally connected
relationships.

Section 1

If you found that your answers were the first choices most
often, you don't interact much with those around you, or
if you do it is in a negative way. You are carrying hostility
and/or resentment in your heart. You are in a bad place
emotionally and would benefit greatly from better connections and some tender love and support. Reach out and
find a group, an activity or friends who can help you feel
more positive about your life and your purpose. You are
too often alone and possibly angry a lot, which puts you
at risk for increased heart issues, high blood pressure and
myriad other physical maladies.

Your challenge is to nurture your emotional well-
being. That will take opening up and connecting to the
people around you. This might feel risky and scary for you
but you need to feel loved and appreciated.

Your anger has been a defense mechanism keeping
you from your deeper feelings of hurt. It is possible you

were hurt as a child or something happened later in life that has made you fearful of closeness. Deep down you still need love and acceptance. Find a loving and self-compassionate way to work through this anger. Hanging on to grudges, anger and hostility will literally kill you.

If you chose the second answer most often, you are disconnected and possibly emotionally shut down. Your challenge is to try to access what is going on in your heart, not just what is going on in your head. For years you have pushed down your emotions to get through the day.

It is possible that, as a child, no one taught you to identify your feelings. Someone probably told you that your feelings weren't important. Maybe your accomplishments were more important to your family than your emotions. This is unfortunately common in our achievement-oriented culture. We tell ourselves that if we are richer, thinner, prettier, we will be happier. Without a sense of our own inner emotional lives, we can't be connected. Your emotional work is to find compassion and tenderness for your own feelings.

Learning to identify what is happening in your heart and body will take time. During several periods during the day, slow down and listen to what thoughts and feelings come to you. When you have suppressed your emotions for a long time, they may all come rushing to the surface at once, which may be overwhelming for you.

Emotions are a normal and important part of life. Feeling them can be intense and hard to handle. Feel comforted that emotions are felt in a bell curve: they build and eventually subside. Both positive and negative emotions are felt this way. Unless you were taught as a child to feel safe about feeling, many of you are frightened of intense emotions. But you *will* make it through such strong emotions.

You may have to spend some time mourning the time you have lost being out of touch with your inner life. Reach out to someone you feel safe with and share your emotional experience of reconnecting to your inner life. You will be healthier and happier as a result.

If you chose the last answer most often, you are doing well. You are emotionally connected with those around you and you feel safe in your world. This is positive for your overall well-being. You are not carrying emotional pain around. You have healthy emotional outlets, like sharing your day and your inner life with the people around you. You are not afraid of emotional vulnerability and you have the courage to feel and say what is really going on for you. Stay connected and enjoy life!

Section 2

"Yes" answers indicate that your intimate relationship is in good shape. Even if the best answer was more like "Most of the time" or "Quite a bit" rather than an unequivocal "yes," you are still enjoying a close relationship that reinforces your well-being.

Section 3

Certain habits creep into a stress-filled life. A compulsive need to have a cell phone nearby all the time—even at meals with a partner or children—suggests that you need to disconnect from the gadgets and connect with people. A compulsive need to snack, even when you're not hungry, sends the same sort of message.

It's possible to laugh out loud when you're all alone watching a television program or a movie, for example. However, sharing a laugh with someone puts you in a high-energy rhythm with another person; if "laughter is the best medicine" then sharing a laugh has the potential to heal two people at once!

And as for the highs and lows of your day, the salient factor is whether or not they involved someone else. If your big regret was not doing the dishes before you left for work, forget it. If your big regret was forgetting to say "happy birthday" to a co-worker, de-stress yourself: Call him or send him a text message.

Think through your highs and lows and realize how they do or don't reflect the connections you have with other people. Consider how people share your joys and play a part in lessening your stress.

HEALING HEART DISEASE

Suzanne Steinbaum, the cardiologist who serves as director of Women and Heart Disease at Lenox Hill Hospital in New York, cites sixteen major indicators of susceptibility to heart disease. She calls them Heart Throbs. They are factors you would expect to be in the mix: body fat, alcohol consumption, smoking, diet and so on. You can start to reverse the ill effects of bad lifestyle choices such as these immediately, but you probably won't get noticeable results immediately. Ironically, the most significant factor is one that you can not only eliminate quickly, but by doing so, you also get *immediate* results. It is stress. Steinbaum notes:

> *Stress affects everything. I mean that. Literally everything in your life can be negatively impacted by too much stress. It might just be the most pervasive and significant Heart Throb you can actually control, because managing it smartly will help you make better decisions about how you really want to live your life. Nothing works well when you are stressed. When you feel calm and in control, everything works better.*

*We've only recently begun to understand how
drastically stress impacts the body, especially in terms of
inflammation. High levels of stress hormones can eventually cause inflammation in the body, leading to high blood
pressure, obesity, and many other Heart Throbs.*[16]

As we explained in chapter 3, stress hormones flood your body when you are in a state of fight or flight, which can result from a threat at work as well as from the approach of a mugger in a dark alley. Co-regulation—the phenomenon of rhythmically connecting with another person who makes you feel safe—immediately arouses calming influences to counter those stress hormones. It works as fast as a sudden shower washing soot off the pavement.

Also in chapter 3, we introduced University of Virginia psychologist Dr. James Coan and his study on the effect of a positive connection with another human being on the fear response. To reiterate briefly, using functional magnetic resonance imaging (fMRI) to track their brain activity, Coan administered small electric shocks to sixteen married women whenever they saw an "X" flash before them. The women's brains lit up to indicate a strong fear response when they felt the shock and were alone. The response diminished when strangers held their hands. It fell substantially when holding the hands of their husbands. It follows that the women in the happiest relationships felt the most relief. This is a dramatic example of co-regulation.[17]

When we spoke with Coan early in 2013, he had just completed a follow-up experiment in cooperation with Susan Johnson, the developer of Emotionally-Focused Therapy (EFT). They took couples in a very distressed state whose relationships seemed toxic to both members of the couple and put them through the handholding experiment. Again, the shocks were administered while one person was alone, with her partner and with a stranger. In this case, Coan did not observe the "handholding effect" with the couples the first time he conducted the experiment. In fact, in some cases, the partner experiencing the shock responded with an even greater sense of threat.[18]

Susan Johnson worked with the couples using EFT. After twenty weeks of EFT, the handholding effect was restored for many of them. In a figurative sense, we could say that they were once again in each other's hearts. In a literal sense, they were able to affect a de-stressing, and therefore a healing, response in each other's hearts.

The process that occurred encompasses three main stages. The first is de-escalation, which involves taking down the level of distress. It involves validating everyone's feelings, particularly the anxious pursuer, and getting that person to a place where he or she feels heard and understood.[19]

The second is deepening the de-escalation so the couple gets to a place of hearing each other instead of talking at each other. It involves the blamer softening and the withdrawer re-engaging. This is the anxious one (blamer) taking the needy pursuit of affection and desire to solve problems down a notch and the avoidant one (withdrawer) perking up a bit about the possibilities in the relationship. This second stage involves a validation of the blamer's anger. EFT therapists call it "bringing the elevator down" because the conversation centers on what's behind the anger.[20] With that being aired, almost invariably the person's anger liquefies and the pool we see is composed of frustration and hurt. It took shape over time due to feeling as though the other partner was not emotionally available. The blamer yells and accuses as a response to not being heard and understood.

The beginning of the change event is the softening of the blamer. The subsequent re-engagement of the withdrawer, or avoidant one, usually centers on getting that person to feel safe. For a while, that person hadn't known when a door would slam or an angry scream would come from the bedroom. The withdrawer had become like a turtle, head inside the shell. In stage two of the EFT process, the turtle takes a peek at what's outside the shell.

It's certainly possible to have two blamers and two withdrawers, too. The fact is, that's just not a common scenario. Attack-attack is tough to sustain, because it takes so much energy for two people to attack each other constantly. Johnson considered one of the couples who participated in the Coan-Johnson study a pair of withdrawers. In their case, the distress probably came out of a total lack of passion. They were like a couple of roommates who got along sometimes, but mostly just went on about their business and co-existed.[21]

Toward the end of stage two, an EFT therapist looks for a "change moment." Usually, it is initiated with the blamer asking for his or her needs to be met. It is a genuine expression of vulnerability and an invitation to get closer that's communicated in a subtle way. With the avoidant partner responding emotionally, the couple arrives at stage three, the point that Johnson calls a "hold me tight conversation."[22]

Trevor has observed many times what happens next to her clients in stage three. The couple starts talking about their future together. "Yeah, we want to buy a boat and go fishing on the river on weekends!" They start to see themselves as a couple again.

Sometimes a couple is not capable of getting to that moment. Sometimes, no matter how closely they follow the path toward understanding "felt sense" of an emotion and the value of vulnerability, there really is no future together for them. It could be that one of them draws a deep line in the sand and says, "I will never be hurt again," which blocks the possibility of feeling vulnerable. And without that, there is no felt sense of love as described at the beginning of this chapter. We know someone who feels this way, who will not trust any creature except her dog. We worry what will happen to her with the unavoidable death of her dog.

In EFT terms, the couples who cannot make it, whether it is limping or leaping, toward a mutual sense of vulnerability cannot have the "hold me tight conversation." So Coan and Johnson could document success with a significant portion of the distressed couples, but there were those who continued to "fail" the handholding experiment.

The healing shift that occurred in the course of EFT might most simply be described as guiding the couples to live from the heart. And in this case, we use *heart* in both the sense of an organ and a symbol of emotion.

They learned to live in greater synchronicity with each other, with their heart rhythms quite literally matching at times. This is the healing phenomenon of co-regulation from an organic perspective.

They also moved away from a transactional method of experiencing their relationships; they started living from the heart by putting feeling first instead of leading with analysis and judgment.

Chapter 7

Criteria for Love

In all of its ninety-four episodes over six years, the TV show *Sex and the City* covered the topic of what people use as their criteria for love. At one point, protagonist Carrie Bradshaw asks herself a question that everyone should ask—or at least some variation of it—to establish if one of your criteria is so negative it undermines the connection with the other person: "Did I ever really love Big or was I addicted to the pain, the exquisite pain, of wanting someone so unattainable?"[1]

Carrie has plenty of company in her confusion over the criteria for love, which is one reason the show lasted as long as it did. For example, Trevor's friend Kim married a hologram. For fifteen years, she was married to someone who actually never existed. She had a person in her head who was ethical, kind and a great business manager. In her mind, he was a great father and a man with a brilliant mind who could figure out how to make life rich (literally and figuratively) for her and her children.

None of it was true. This man was a product of her imagination and hope. Her criteria for love centered on smart, caring, competent and ethical, so when she had the chemistry that supported her falling for someone, she simply fantasized that he was all of those things. The result of not being tuned in to her reality meant that, on a day-to-day basis, her felt sense was fear. She was always worried about stepping out of line; after all, if he was such a great person, anything that went wrong had to be her fault—right?

Thinking back on this, Kim now calls that relationship "a marriage of still face," meaning that she was like the baby described in chapter 1 who did not receive the feedback needed to feel safe and loved. Yet for the sake of her children, she continued in the marriage until it became unbearable for her and the children. The harsh reality is that none of her criteria for love had been met.

Identifying your criteria for love, therefore, is only half the challenge in developing and sustaining a strong connection with someone. Those criteria cannot just disappear from your emotional radar screen once they are met—or you *think* they have been met. They serve as energetic reminders of why you are with someone.

When you respect these criteria as a vital part of the health of your relationships, brain-imaging can prove to you that you feel linked to people you love. It can prove that those people take down your stress level so your immune system can do an optimal job of protecting and restoring your health.

IN SICKNESS AND IN HEALTH

When Emily first met Rob, she found him very attractive. They dated for a few months and she enjoyed his disarming honesty and his ability to fix just about anything, even the hem on her skirt. When Emily's housemate met him, she said, "He's a definite keeper!" Emily asked her why. "Just look at him!" He was the most handsome man either of them had ever seen outside of movie stars.

About two years into their marriage, Emily developed a chronic skin rash, had started smoking cigarettes and regularly drank too much wine at dinner. A former competitive athlete, she now stayed at the office too long, almost never went to the gym and was fully immersed in co-dependent life with Rob.

Four years into the marriage, Emily was among those at her company who were laid off. The day her boss traveled from headquarters to her office in order to fire her, she felt a strange sense of relief and anticipation. The very next day, she went to a building with some executive suites downtown and rented an office for the consulting business she'd decided to launch. She reconnected with some good friends who supported her in giving up cigarettes and working out at the gym again.

A few months into the process of reclaiming her health and her career, she realized that she and Rob seemed very separate. Without their co-dependent lifestyle intact, he spent more time getting stoned with friends and she spent more time with her new colleagues, clients and gym buddies.

One day, she came home and said she wanted to do a little experiment suggested on a self-help tape about relationships. She asked Rob to list five things in order of priority: love, joy, excitement, success and security.

Here is Rob's list, in the order of importance:

- Security
- Happiness
- Love
- Excitement
- Success

Emily's list differed:

- Success
- Excitement
- Love
- Happiness
- Security

They were completely opposite. Rob and Emily made a lame attempt at both individual and couple's therapy and then divorced.

Their list of priorities hints at how they felt about love at the time, but says more about their attachment styles and the transactional nature of their relationship. Rob was an anxious pursuer who wanted Emily to give him security, happiness and love. He didn't really focus on excitement or security, because they were priorities that "belonged" to Emily. Emily was avoidant and dismissive. She craved success and excitement, which she felt were results she could create without Rob, and she assumed love, happiness and security would be in her life if she took care of her top two priorities.

What were their criteria for love? They both had them—we all do—but to a great extent they ignored them during the process of getting to know each other. The fact is, Emily and Rob may never have been in love, or perhaps only had a fleeting experience of it. They were strongly attracted to each other and liked a few things about each other's talents and qualities. However, for the most part, they were two people whose heart rhythms were never in synch.

As we discussed earlier, there is a causal link between love and health. With the deterioration of Emily's health, we again see that a relationship that is supposed to embody love on a day-to-day basis—but is instead a prolonged case of hooking up—causes disease. We presented this scenario from Emily's point of view, but the reality is that, in the course of the relationship, Rob's well-being took a nosedive, too. In the last two years of that marriage, he was hospitalized three times.

For Emily, Rob was the human equivalent of junk food: a scrumptious, intoxicating treat that was bad for her heart in all senses. Unfortunately, choosing someone who makes us sick is all too common. Self-image issues, family-of-origin issues, and input from people around us can all help shape our understanding of love and criteria for it. For example, Emily had thought of herself as an ugly duckling growing up, so being with a handsome man was an affirmation. Her family felt an important criterion was that he be Catholic; he was. All her friends liked him and gave her positive feedback, so she concluded he must be as wonderful inside and outside as she thought he was.

It's very easy to do what Emily and Rob did, but it's also relatively easy to make a healthy choice. First, consider how easy it is to get involved in a relationship that potentially undermines health.

Meeting someone who excites us can put us into a state of fight-or-flight just as though we were threatened. And in a real way, when we meet someone we think might be "the one," we do feel a bit threatened because we know we are vulnerable. Recall what happens when we're in that state: the cognitive brain shuts down and our automatic responses take over. We may not even be capable of being in touch mentally and emotionally with our criteria for love on a first date—depending on how hot it is. And if that chemistry continues, it really could be years before the couple wakes up to their diseased reality.

To some degree, you create a hologram of a person to whom you're attracted, because you don't really know him yet. Regardless of the feeling of love at first sight, or the confidence that the dating website did a great job of matching you, you really don't know the person in a full-bodied (or full-hearted) sense, so your imagination fills in the gaps.

In the early stages of a relationship, even the most avoidant person may be quite demonstrative, even to the extent of acting like an anxious pursuer. It isn't until later in the relationship, when both parties start settling into their grooves, that the attachment style will surface. The hologram will start to become a tangible being with discernible features and at that point it will be possible to figure out if the person really does meet your criteria for love. It's also possible to remain oblivious to what is in front of you and continue to sustain the holographic image.

We certainly don't mean to dismiss the phenomenon of love at first sight because it can be genuine and well-grounded in your criteria for love. That flash that "this is the one" may well be a realization that you have what you want in terms of how safe you feel, how well you connect with the person's values and how excited you get when you are close to the person. That person seems somehow familiar to you because what you want in a relationship was grooved into your head a long time before.

One element of feeling secure with someone is how much like you the person is. One of the enthusiastic remarks someone will make just after meeting a person who is simpatico with them is, "He's just like me!" or "We have so much in common!" or "She really gets me!" No matter how it's said, it means the same thing, which is the opposite of the dismissive, "He totally doesn't get me." That initial blush of chemistry and connection reflects the most common criterion for love. It is the first stage of attunement. You're excited, connected and you want to be even closer than you are at the moment.

Attunement means you are listening, feeling and becoming aware of your partner's experiences and feelings. Being attuned means you are proactive, too: You ask about how he or she is feeling. You find out what is happening in that person's life from a non-defensive, non-judgmental place. You make it safe for your partner to talk about deep-seated fears, hurts and experiences. Lack of attunement in a relationship can easily lead to attachment injuries, or make it extremely difficult for a partner to cope with attachment injuries. We explore further how attunement works in chapter 9.

Being available emotionally doesn't mean you need to solve the other person's problems. You just need to be there and listen empathetically. By doing this, you show that you care, love and have concern for your partner. That is attunement.

Maryann is friends with a couple that has had sixty-five years of attunement. That doesn't mean they get along perfectly all the time, of course. As Trevor's friend and EFT trainer, George Faller, says often about connections, "All you have to do is get it right about 33 percent of the time." It means that even successful, securely attached couples can have times when they disagree and moments when they don't want to be in the same room together. But about one-third of the time, they are invested in bringing each other joy or at least a sense of security.

Gayle and Bill, the couple Maryann knows, met right after World War II at a Navy base. They married within months and raised two lovely daughters. They are consistently thoughtful about the way they speak and listen to each other. So it never occurred to Maryann that there might be times when they raised their voices and got critical.

One afternoon at his home, Bill sat in his favorite chair and looked out at the yard. One of the trees had been trimmed back such that he could see a corner of the neighbor's garage. "Darling, did you tell the gardener to take some of the limbs off that oak tree?" His tone was moderately sharp.

"Yes, I did. I thought they might fall if we had a big storm."

"I told you I did not want any trimming that forced me to look at the horrible garage next door!" This time, even though Bill was elderly, his voice carried a great deal of power.

Maryann quietly approached Gayle in the kitchen to offer support. Humming a tune, she looked at Maryann quizzically. "Just because he raised his voice doesn't make him a bad man," Gayle said calmly. And then she went on singing as she prepared dinner.

Shortly after that, Bill said, "Darling, I'm sorry I raised my voice to you."

"I accept your apology, my dear. "She said. And then she smiled at him, "There's always a first time and I'm sure it will never happen again." There was a little wink in the way she teased him. Sure, this kind of thing had to have happened at least a few times in their sixty-five years of marriage. But they were so attuned, so securely attached, that they knew when and how to cut each other a break.

That's how people end up being able to celebrate their union, whether it's sixty-five days or sixty-five years.

ATTACHMENT INJURIES, PLEASURES AND HEALING

Susan Johnson, who developed EFT, coined the term "attachment injury" to describe a violation of a key expectation in an intimate relationship. She explains it as follows:

> *"An attachment injury is characterized by an abandonment or by a betrayal of trust during a critical moment of need. The injurious incident defines the relationship as insecure and maintains relationship distress because it is continually used as a standard for the dependability of the offending partner."*[2]

For one couple, it may be infidelity, but another couple might not consider straying sexually as an attachment injury. There is no list of bad behaviors that would constitute attachment injuries for any and every couple. People on the outside of a couple looking into their relationship might be aghast at some of the behaviors that each tolerates. But unless those behaviors meet the criteria of making someone feel unsafe—psychologically and/or physically—on an ongoing basis, then the couple is not dealing with an attachment injury.

The concept of "expectation" is central to determining whether or not something is an attachment injury. When two people enter into an intimate relationship, they have a sense of what they expect the other person to be like on a day-to-day basis. It amounts to a sense of entitlement about how each will treat the other, as well as the person's friends, family and anyone else who's important. It also involves how the partner treats him or herself. Essentially, they reflect respect for a partner and everything and everyone that is important to that person.

Every relationship has entitlements woven through it. They reflect your vision of what contributes to the quality of your life and the health of your relationship. Some of the expectations may be articulated in the form of marriage vows, but many of them may not actually be voiced until a violation occurs.

When writing their book *Date Decoder*, Maryann and her co-author, Greg Hartley, interviewed a number of people of all ages in relationships about their "deal breaker" entitlements. These are what Trevor would, for the most part, put in the category of potential attachment injuries. In order of importance, here are two lists, one a synthesis of what male respondents told Maryann and Greg and the other a synthesis of what female respondents said.[3]

MALE
Deal Breakers
    Drug addiction
    Sudden religious fanaticism

Infidelity
Disrespect of family
Theft
Habitual deception
Lack of sex or bad sex
Abusive behavior

Violations of Expectations, but not necessarily deal breakers
Lack of self-esteem (letting herself go)
Carelessness about the home
Overdependence
Deliberate unemployment

FEMALE
Deal Breakers
Abusive (violent behavior)
Disrespect of family
Disrespect of friends
Trivializing career
Habitual deception
Dismissive behavior
Harsh treatment of others
Lack of backbone

Violation of Expectations, but not necessarily deal breakers
Choice of conflicting lifestyle
Infidelity
Lack of sex or bad sex
Lack of self-esteem (letting himself go)[4]

We invite you to review the answers with the knowledge that these are people in relationships, so presumably they care about their partners. With that in mind, a response like "drug addiction" is not a condemnation of illegal or immoral behavior, but an expression

that the partner who has an addiction problem is a self-abuser—
someone who becomes unlovable, perhaps, because she doesn't
love herself.

Now, consider some of the responses in light of what you now
know about attachment styles. Given that it is often true that couples
are composed of an anxious pursuer who is female and an avoidant
dismissive male, it is not surprising that we see violations such as
"abusive behavior" and "overdependence" on the male side. It suggests
that the men who responded had some prior or current exposure to
an anxious pursuer—often someone whose blaming behavior might
easily be seen as abusive.

On the female side, the high placement of "disrespect" and
"dismissive behavior" suggests that the women who provided input
had some current or prior negative experiences with avoidant dismissive types.

Cindy's experience was an extreme example of the kind of dismissive behavior that causes attachment injuries. Her mother had
passed away weeks after her marriage to John. Soon after that, he got a
new opportunity in England so the two of them moved there and had
a baby within the first year of their marriage.

Cindy felt very alone, with her husband working long hours and
herself trying to cope with a new baby as well as the move to a foreign
country. The mother-in-law moved in, ostensibly to help out with the
baby. She immediately began criticizing Cindy for her breastfeeding
and other aspects of her parenting. John sided with his mother.

Cindy's milk dried up the day that happened.

Fifteen years later when the couple sought therapy, Cindy still
cried when she thought about what had happened. John was extremely avoidant; he did not see how much damage he had done to
her for quite a long time. Eventually, he came to understand and felt
absolutely terrible about what he'd done, but "undoing" it to rebuild
trust took a great deal of work. It was no surprise that Cindy had thick
barriers to allowing herself to feel vulnerable with him.

When it comes to attachment injuries, we are talking about
massive open sores that cause one or both members of a couple to feel

a great need to shield him or herself from the other—to put up a non-porous emotional barrier just to stop the pain from coming in.

Many challenges common to couples can engender attachment injuries. Unlike infidelity or lying, sometimes events outside of the control of the couple give rise to attachment injuries because of how one or the other responds to the event. For example, a miscarriage can represent one of the most significant attachment injuries. Unlike certain other cultures, ours has no ritual to grieve around a miscarriage. Lacking that structure around how to act and what to say, friends, family members and even a partner may avoid touching on the issue at all. That's an isolating experience that only deepens the painful aloneness the miscarriage may have caused.

Another circumstance that often leads to attachment injuries is serious illness or a catastrophic accident. At a time when intimate relationships should play a central role in restoring health, they can actually worsen the person's condition. Again, the person may already feel isolated due to a devastating diagnosis or trauma, but that may just be the beginning of the story. The healthy partner may feel just as isolated, as well as guilty and helpless, in the face of a serious health issue. Rather than come into the relationship with even more commitment and energy, many partners turn their backs on the ugly reality and seek solace elsewhere. The political careers of Newt Gingrich and John Edwards took hits when it surfaced that each of them had cheated on a seriously ill wife. Gingrich had an affair while his wife was battling uterine cancer; Edwards cheated on his wife during her years of fighting breast cancer.[5]

An old attachment injury, unrelated to a current relationship, can also be a wound that has never quite healed and keeps reopening with the slightest nudge. Kathy and Roseanne were dear friends, but once, in the middle of a disagreement over something trivial, Kathy brought up the fact that Roseanne had an abortion. Kathy's self-righteous, judgmental tone of voice was more than Roseanne could take. They never spoke again. Unintentionally, Kathy did Roseanne a big favor because the incident made her realize that the abortion was a trauma from which she had never recovered; she sought therapy.

Healing an attachment injury involves forgiveness; getting to the point of forgiveness, whether for yourself or someone else, can be a complex challenge. Years after Ponzi-scheme genius Bernard Madoff was sentenced to 150 years in prison, many of his family members, former clients and business journalists still asserted they saw no reason to forgive Madoff. At first, looking at some of the articles, Trevor bristled, but in thinking about the nature of forgiveness, particularly in the context of her work with couples, she decided she had to agree with them. People who lost their life savings felt that Madoff had injured them personally. But regardless of any remorseful statement Madoff may have made in court or in public statements about his actions, he didn't look his victims in the eyes and say it to each one. He didn't hear them express the unique pain and anger his abuses had caused them. There was no progression in mutual understanding and caring that would prompt forgiveness.

Penny and Paul are a couple who *do* go through the steps to arrive at forgiveness and begin the healing process after an attachment injury.

Penny was in the hospital room going through a miscarriage. Her husband, Paul, was down the hall talking with her gynecologist and filling out paperwork for the hospital. He thought that he was doing the right thing at the time. She was alone, grieving and desperately needing him.

For a few weeks afterward, he attributed her sour mood to hormone fluctuations and assumed it would just take a while for her mind and body to calm down after the trauma. When the mood persisted and the relationship seemed rocky, they sought therapy. They had to go through several steps to reach a point where forgiveness was possible and could support healing.

Step 1: Validating the anger

Usually the injured person is angry and blaming, so Penny's reaction was to be expected. Trying to shut down the anger abruptly would be dismissive; so it's important to validate it for awhile. The person who has been hurt and carrying the attachment wound has probably been told repeatedly to "get over it." Minimizing her pain and experience would just re-traumatize Penny.

Step 2: Bringing down the emotional elevator

Carrying that anger through a therapy session would get in the way of accomplishing anything, however, so the emotional elevator had to be brought down. Instead of focusing on the anger, Trevor got her to focus on how she felt abandoned at a time of need.

"Timing" and "need" are commonly two of the key ingredients in an attachment injury. It is possible to have a miscarriage and have no trauma associated with it whatsoever. It is possible that the timing for the pregnancy was wrong, so the woman would feel relief. It's also possible for a woman not to experience grief because she had no emotional connection to the pregnancy at that point. She might not feel a desperate need for her partner, as Penny did.

Step 3: Verbalizing the pain

Penny needed to articulate how she felt during the experience that caused the injury. She told Paul, "I was crying. I needed you to be with me. It hurt me that you didn't understand. You didn't see how much I needed you at that moment."

Step 4: Engaging the injurer

After she said that, he had to consider the question: "What is it like to hear her say that?"

Paul had a tendency to be defensive. His first response was, "I had to get that done for insurance purposes. And the doctor was asking me questions so I couldn't just walk away." Paul felt his mission focus was perfectly justified.

This kind of attitude is typically the genesis of attachment injuries. The person who does the hurting gets defensive and dismissive and doesn't acknowledge the hurt he or she caused. Because defenses are up, that blocks the person's ability to sense the level of pain in the other person. The person who did the hurting has to slow down and say, "I get it. I understand what I did to hurt you."

Paul did so, with great sincerity. His own vulnerability began to surface.

Step 5: Arriving at forgiveness

Once that acknowledgement process begins, the couple moves toward a place of forgiveness—but isn't there immediately. The person who was hurt first has to take in what the other partner is expressing. This is not a straightforward exchange of "I apologize," followed by "Okay, I forgive you." That's hollow. Forgiveness comes out of feeling understood, having the emotions connected with the pain acknowledged and appreciated and sensing that the partner is in touch with your pain. It's not just an intellectual grasping of the circumstances, but a felt sense of the hurt that was caused. At that point, it's possible for the injured person to get past the barrier that had been holding her back from trusting in the relationship again.

The last part of the forgiveness dance is the person who did the hurting taking responsibility for what he did and saying, "I'll do my best not to let this happen again."

When Penny heard Paul's message and his intent to make an earnest effort not to repeat such an injury, she could forgive him.

For some people, it's incredibly difficult to do what Penny and Paul did. If you grew up in a family that kept emotional pain bottled up or you had parents who dredged up every bad thing you ever did whenever they were angry with you, then the dance of forgiveness might have a rhythm that seems foreign to you. In the upcoming discussion on couples coding, tune in to how you can take small steps every day to make it easier to "sway to the music" if you ever do face a serious issue as a couple.

The counterbalance to attachment injuries is what we might call attachment pleasures, although you won't find that term in psychological literature. We define attachment pleasures as what you aim to both give and get as part of a loving, secure relationship. This is what couples often talk about in their self-composed marriage vows.

Trevor also has a unique name for the ongoing process of making those attachment pleasures come to life: *couples coding*. These are viscerally felt moments in which one partner tunes into another's feelings and needs and strengthens the bond between them. They may be small and ostensibly insignificant or they could be show-stopping moments that you tell your grandchildren about in years to come.

Couples coding helps prevent attachment injuries as well as support healing after an injury has occurred. It builds trust and is physically restorative. And it can apply to friends, parents and children, or any other two people in a relationship just as much as it does to a couple. Alicia told Trevor that her dearest friend simply made note of the fact she looked unusually distracted. She tried to brush it off with, "Oh, it's nothing. I'm just not in the best of moods today." Not willing to settle for that, the friend gently asked a few questions, and then a few more, until Alicia revealed why she had some fear and dismay wrapped around a particular issue with her boyfriend. He had violated one of her fundamental entitlements by physically threatening her brother. It was not a hurt that she should have kept to herself, for various reasons. In telling Trevor this story, Alicia said she felt so much relief from the conversation with her friend that it brought her clarity. She got the perspective she needed to address the issue with her boyfriend in a constructive way instead of going into the conversation like an anxious blamer—which was her default style. That's couples coding as much as anything similarly transformative that happens in a marriage.

Now let's track one couple from their wedding day through the first year of marriage to suggest how they employed couples coding to heal some of the wounds from past relationships and get their life together off to a secure start. It should be noted that this is a couple in their forties, both with previous marriages behind them, so their turning to counseling reflects some wisdom about how to avert failure in their new relationship.

Courtney and Jake planned a giant, mid-summer wedding with their immediate families, stepfamilies and their many good friends. They were both in their mid-forties and firmly believed everything would go right this time. What they didn't plan for was a family member potentially ruining their big day.

The maid of honor, who was one of Courtney's three sisters, had not arrived at the church and the wedding music was already playing. All the guests were seated, including at least a dozen children under the age of ten. The church was hot; babies were crying. The sister arrived twenty-five minutes after the wedding had been scheduled to start and acted as though nothing was wrong. "Hi, Sweetie, you look gorgeous!" she chirped at Courtney as she grabbed her bouquet of flowers and prepared to walk down the aisle.

The wedding continued but afterwards, a number of guests were rather vocal about the sister's late appearance and nonchalance. "What the heck was she doing?" they wondered.

Courtney's sisters, who were also bridesmaids, seemed utterly confused by the question, or by the implication that their sister had done anything wrong. Her hairstylist had shown up late, they explained. You certainly wouldn't have wanted her to walk down the aisle with bad hair, would you?

Courtney was always the one in the family who kept quiet about her complaints. She was the peacemaker, the neutral party. Everyone else's dramas were more important than hers. No one in her family came to her defense in a dispute, but she grew to see that as normal and stopped caring. That's the way they are, she decided. Her previous marriage had the same dynamics. When her husband had an affair, she turned all her attention to her work and children and simply ignored the problem for almost five years. Courtney had a decidedly avoidant attachment style.

The next day, all the sisters except the one who had served as maid of honor were having coffee. Courtney expressed her hurt at her sister's lateness and, in a very uncustomary display, she flashed some anger about it. The sisters shut her down. "My God, you're selfish! What did you expect her to do? It wasn't her fault the hairdresser didn't show up on time."

"Selfish?" Courtney screamed. "It was my wedding day. It was about me and Jake, not her!"

At that moment, Jake walked into the room. He had never heard her that upset, so he knew it could not be minimized. Looking at all of the sisters, he stood up for Courtney and said that what had happened the day before was not something they could ignore; it would have to stop. He told Courtney he found her sister's behavior hurtful as well and that he was going to call her that minute and tell her. When he did, Courtney felt, for the first time, that a member of her family had her back. He respected her feelings and stood shoulder to shoulder with her so they could handle the problem as a couple.

She felt safe and validated. Her whole life, Courtney's parents had acted as though her feelings didn't matter. They oiled the squeaky wheels and she had always moved along politely. At that point, she knew the marriage was right. She was no longer a "one" who had to take care of herself because nobody else would. She was a "one" that included a partner who honored her emotions; they would take care of each other.

Checking back with this couple a few months later, we wondered what other examples they had of couples coding. We want to point out that sometimes these viscerally perceived moments just flow out of the normal course of interaction. They are simply random acts of kindness. Sometimes, however, they are created deliberately. They are like a conscious renewal of the vow to love and honor with one partner "bothering" to invest the time and energy to pay close attention to what will make the other partner feel safe and validated.

Here are two examples of both of them initiating couples coding:

- Jake knew Courtney would be working until 6:30 P.M. one night and saw that she was a little stressed as she checked the fridge that morning. He said simply, "I'll handle the kids' dinner tonight." He saw the stress drain from her face and body and she sighed a big "thank you!" She's a doer; she wouldn't have asked for or expected this. Couples coding is about paying attention and making an offer like Jake did. When that happens over and over, Courtney will develop a habit of trust. She will know Jake stands ready and willing to help her—whether she's busy, sad or sick.

- Courtney is a very bright woman with a business degree and a good deal of corporate experience. She invited a business conversation with Jake one day because she noticed that his pre-occupation with his company seemed out of balance. Rather than try to lure him back to family interaction, she focused squarely on the thing that was taking him away from it. It helped him in a pragmatic way in terms of finding a way forward with his team, as well as in an energetic way. Courtney's action had the same kind of effect as the one described in chapter 6: When we share the load psychologically and emotionally with another person, we literally use less energy than when we try to go it alone. It worked for the NBA teams that researchers studied and it worked for the people in Jim Coan's research regarding their abilities to climb a hill.

Trevor often sees change moments in therapy that come out of couples coding. When a distressed couple that loves each other pays attention to their connection, that kind of behavior engenders a sense of joy and hope.

Couples coding is a practical, attachment-healing activity that belongs in every close connection we have. The more you do it consciously, the more you will find yourself doing it reflexively. Once it becomes an element of your life, you have found the path toward co-regulation and genuine trust that allows for health-sustaining and health-restoring emotional bonds.

Here is a short questionnaire to help you determine just how difficult it might be for you and your partner to do some couples coding. These four questions simply focus on your attention on how you talk to and about your partner.

Questionnaire on Conversation Style

One big aspect of couples coding is how you relate to one another. Here are some questions to help you examine the quality of your interactions.

When your spouse/partner tells a story to friends in your presence and messes up some details:
  a) You interrupt, using a condescending tone and correct your spouse right then and there.
  b) You let it go; the story was mostly true and those details don't really matter.
  c) You don't even notice; you tuned out since you have heard the story a million times before.

When you tell friends a story about your spouse/partner, the story is about:
  a) Something your spouse did that was really funny and stupid and you imply the question, "How could she/he have messed up so badly?"
  b) Something your spouse did that made you proud.
  c) You don't tell stories about him/her; there's nothing much to say.

Take a few minutes to think about the majority of your interactions and consider the tone in which you speak to each other. Is it:
  a) Angry?

    b) Playful/caring?
    c) Condescending?

You have a skill in a particular area, say, gardening. Your partner is outside of his/her skill area, yet offers a suggestion on gardening. How does that go?
    a) You give an order, "We'll do it my way, since I know what I'm doing."
    b) You express openness to your partner's idea and may even act on it.
    c) You nod in a perfunctory manner and give a rather dismissive, disinterested response.

If you chose the first option most times, you don't have much respect for your spouse—and that very likely goes both ways. This is something you want to examine at a deeper level. Something is going wrong where you are feeling hurt or distanced from your spouse and you use your words as little knives to cut him or her down. This is terrible for both your relationship and your immune systems: You are physically wearing each other out!

- Couples coding for you might start by listening and watching. You are in "push" mode; try simply going neutral and watching how your partner responds to situations, conversations, challenges and fun.

If you usually picked the second option, you feel connected and you communicate to your spouse and those around you that you have high regard for them. This is positive and supportive of your emotional and physical well-being.

- Employ couples coding as a way to keep the enjoyment high and provide powerful healing energy if you face difficult times.

If you selected the last option most often, you are disconnected and avoidant. You are feeling hurt but you don't acknowledge your own hurt or your partner's feelings. You need to do deeper work as well to heal the distance between you.

- Couples coding for you might start by reading body language. Look for cues that tell you what your partner is feeling. (Review chapter 4 for ideas.)

In general, consider your own sensitivities about how your partner speaks to you and about you. As painful as it may be to admit it, sometimes the comments that provoke the strongest anger, the most defensive behavior or the most retaliatory remarks are those that are true, at least in part. If your partner suggests that you were deceitful about something and you know in your heart you were not, and would not be, deceitful, how would you react? Disbelief, probably. The remark doesn't hit a nerve because it isn't about you. You might question how or why that person came to such a conclusion but the comment is essentially absurd. On the other hand, those sharp remarks that send cortisol and adrenaline surging through your body may sound especially horrible because something about them is true. Couples coding requires that you become more aware of the truth and fiction in your conversations with your partner.

IDENTIFYING AND ENERGIZING YOUR CRITERIA FOR LOVE

Everyone is yearning to belong, to be valued and to be safe. That is what secure attachment is, so we might say that everyone is yearning to develop and/or maintain a secure attachment style. When we seek a partner in life, we are somehow trying to find the person that will fulfill this desire.

Despite this, it is not uncommon for a man or a woman to plunge into a relationship with desire for excitement and intrigue. Craving a taste of an exciting James Bond-style romance is fueled by pop culture. But pop culture should not help us settle on our criteria for love or we'll end up in some distorted TV-style world where we are actors pretending to be in love, not real people who really are in love.

It's also not uncommon for someone who has gone through a failed relationship to form criteria that run counter to what she just experienced. Sometimes that works and sometimes it doesn't; it really depends on what made the earlier relationship come together. In *Sex and the City*, when Charlotte marries Dr. Trey MacDougal, she has the handsome, Christian, well-bred, highly educated companion of her dreams—but she ends up being miserable. She turns around and marries her bald, slightly overweight, Jewish divorce lawyer who puts his used tea bags on furniture—and ends up being deliriously happy. The one criterion she held on to was that she wanted to have a husband who would help her create a family. Finding Harry Goldblatt, the opposite of Trey, was a good thing for Charlotte.[6]

That's often not the case. Choosing to explore a relationship with someone because of what he or she is not, rather than strengthening your emotional core by focusing on your authentic criteria for love, does not bode well for a relationship.

Angie began counseling on her doctor's orders. An athletic, beautiful woman in her mid-forties, she got some bad results back after a routine physical. Mild hypertension and a dangerous rise in her bad cholesterol level were two results her general practitioner targeted as indicative of a problem. She told her physician that she went to the gym regularly, often went for short runs and ate well.

Angie's doctor was aware of the research documenting a link between a person's reaction to stress and lipid levels. This is an individual thing, so it isn't possible to say that x amount of stress always results in *y* rise in bad cholesterol. The correlation is there, however, even though the effect varies from person to person. Knowing that, her physician urged her to begin psychotherapy to talk about what was going on in her life.

As Angie spoke to Trevor about her situation, it became clear that she was an avoidant person who talked around issues. Her primary reasons for being in her marriage, which was already past the fifteen-year mark, were financial security for her and her children, someone who didn't stray from her sexually and who periodically expressed his passion for her. We might say these were her criteria for love. Rather than identifying what she felt would help a strong connection take shape, however, she settled on criteria that reflected what went wrong with her first marriage. Unfortunately, in addition to getting what she asked for, she also got an alcoholic husband who was sometimes abusive.

What she hoped to find with Trevor was the answer to her most stressful question: "Is staying with him the best thing for my children?"

As she talked, tears welled up in her eyes. She kept on side-stepping questions about how she felt, even though anyone looking at her would see that her situation was sad and difficult. She sucked in the tears and backed up a bit and said, "Yes, but this is really about doing the right thing for the kids." Avoidant people use maneuvers like this to distance themselves from their own feelings.

She made a breakthrough in learning about "bottom-up processing": first identifying the emotions she was feeling, and then describing what they did to her physically. Once she got some words to hook onto what was happening for her, she started sobbing.

She reconnected mentally and emotionally with the reason she was in therapy. It was because she was sick. Her relationship had made her sick. The question she had to explore was not, "What's best for the kids?" but "What needs to happen so I can be healthy again?"

In general, therapists try to remain optimistic about couples staying together. When it's clear that the factors that brought them together really are not about love—they are criteria for an acceptable, transactional union—then it's time to admit that their sticking together may be a flawed concept.

Angie now faces a very tough set of choices. If she honestly believes that maintaining the status quo is the best course of action for her children, she will be choosing a life that could kill her.

Establish criteria for love with a focus on what it will take to cultivate a secure attachment. Knowing you want to be with someone who values having children is important. Knowing you want to be with someone who manages money well can be just as important. It depends on your values and priorities, and it depends on what kind of behavior reinforces a sense of trust.

Pay attention to your body and exactly what you feel when your partner does certain things that remind you of a criterion for love. Let's say you treasure expressions of respect for your competence. When your partner takes the time to focus on something you accomplished, asks you questions about it and shows genuine interest and caring about that success, where do you feel it? How do you feel it? Do you feel so deeply energized that you would say it's on the cellular level? You know at that moment that your partner has met a criterion for love.

The converse is also true. Think about what happens to you in a state of stress. For many of Trevor's friends, they tense their shoulders. The shoulders actually rise up and the muscles in their necks get tight. For Trevor it's her stomach. When she gets nervous she can't eat and, in fact, she doesn't even feel hungry. That "knot" in her gut is tight; there is no room for food. These are signals from the body—responding to environmental stimuli—that emotional upset has invaded. When you feel something like that and the cause is your partner, give some thought to your criteria for love. Did your partner just do something, or neglect to do something, that you consider vitally important to the health of your connection?

With compassion, see where you are in the moment and then express it. Particularly if you're avoidant, your responsibility is to tell your partner figuratively where you are and what you are feeling.

If you are an anxious pursuer, your responsibility is to take a deep breath and don't scream, yell, blame or criticize. Step back from the pursuit for a few moments and pay attention to your partner as well as yourself. Are you feeling lonely or abandoned? If so, what do you need to not feel that way? Keep in mind that screaming pushes your partner further away, rather than bringing him or her closer to you. What signals is your partner giving you? Again, like the couple who had a major change event in therapy when she simply complimented her husband, look at the person's face. Remember the face-heart connection.

CHAPTER 8

Criteria for Security

The sweet spot in relationships is shared vulnerability, which allows each person in the relationship to be authentic. The importance of vulnerability in feeling secure spotlights a paradox; at least it does if we use common images of security, which involve barriers and occlusion. Vulnerability requires barrier removal and emotional porosity.

In addition to connoting some kind of barrier, security has a dirty reputation; it is often used synonymously with complacency or perceived as a "safety net" of some kind. Reframing its importance in terms of relationships—giving it a positive connotation in this society—is one goal of this book.

If we experience love as we have defined it (chapter 6) on a daily basis, it gives us a tremendous sense of security. When it's gone, it's a scary feeling; suddenly the security is gone. Part of the work in a relationship is paying attention to changes that reinforce the sense of security and those that rob us of it. We have to be *aware* that we have it when we have it, as well as to recognize a disconnect when it doesn't seem to be there or is truly gone.

HOW DO YOU FEEL COMFORTED?

Donna is a sculptor, quite active in her profession at the age of eighty. Knowing that a major snowstorm was on the way, she still decided to drive nearly 200 miles to a gallery opening where several of her pieces would be featured. As the flakes fell, the snow became so dense she could barely see. Her heart raced and she felt herself clutching the steering wheel. Seeing two semi-trailer trucks just ahead in the right lane, she inched toward them and then maneuvered her car right between them. She felt herself instantly relax; the rest of the drive involved a lot less stress for her.

Being wedged between two semis in a snowstorm would put most people's sympathetic nervous system into overdrive. This story spotlights the point that different people can have very different criteria for feeling safe, yet the effects are identical: the internal and external signs of the fight-or-flight state dissipate.

The story also differentiates between the kind of self-generated sense of security that relates to Donna's situation and the kind that has relevance for the discussion here. The security that we are focused on occurs in relation to others. It is not an individual experience, but rather is inextricably linked to your healthy, loving connections. It is knowing there is someone there for you, knowing you are not alone, knowing someone understands you. Security fostered by a relationship makes you feel grounded and at peace. From a practical perspective, it helps you digest your food. The reason is that security helps you achieve a state of homeostasis, that is, an ability to maintain internal equilibrium by adjusting, moment by moment, to meet the needs of your body.

In Danny's story, explicit gratitude is a main criterion for security.

Danny's father and mother were negligent; he was failing ninth grade when his basketball coach invited him to live at his home. Danny felt so estranged from his biological parents that he even took the last name of the couple who gave him a home. The coach's wife stayed on top of him about homework and household responsibilities; she and her husband, perhaps in a literal way, had saved his life.

When Danny and his wife, Ann, had twin boys, they became his primary focus in life. He became overly functional with his sons, particularly as it pertained to schoolwork—meaning he made sure they did their homework, were ready for pop quizzes and took on extra-credit projects whenever teachers suggested them.

In therapy sessions, Danny got very tense when speaking about his oversight of the boys because he felt that Ann did not appreciate how much effort he put into parenting.

She was over-functioning as well, but in her case most of the energy and focus went into her career. Ann made more money than Danny and in therapy would express criticism and sometimes disgust that he didn't do enough at home—except his excessive attention to the kids.

Danny felt she didn't appreciate or notice what he did, whether it was for the boys or related to anything else. He felt like a failure and under constant threat.

Finally, they got to a point in a session where Ann said, "I do see what you do with our children and I appreciate it." She was not a woman who handed out unqualified compliments. Generally, a statement like that would be followed by, "...but..." Understandably, all that Danny ever heard was the "but" and whatever came after it, like "...but you leave dirty dishes in the sink" or "...but you gave the boys peanut butter and jelly sandwiches three times last week."

So when Ann stopped after simply expressing appreciation, Danny was shocked.

His face and demeanor changed dramatically. His body language suddenly conveyed so much relaxation and joy that he almost looked like a different person. It was a vivid illustration of a heart-face connection.

Even Ann observed, "Your face looks so different!" Her compassion and acknowledgment caused him to feel secure with her at that moment and the expression of how he felt immediately went to his face. Up to that point, she hadn't realized what a deep influence she had on him: With just a few words, she triggered an emotional transformation.

Another realization quickly followed. Ann hadn't wanted to snuggle with him because his demeanor was off-putting. He was constantly tense because he didn't trust that she could and would be kind to him. Seeing this "different person" made her want to pull him closer to her. Even his energy was different. They hugged. And, for that moment at least, he felt safe with her. It was a step toward creating an equilibrium and secure attachment in their marriage.

Addiction is about finding a state of equilibrium without reliance on anyone else. Addiction is what EFT therapists would call an "artificial attachment." It is a source of comfort, a stress reliever that essentially simulates co-regulation. You feel stressed and grab the glass of wine; you feel better. The stress goes away—except it doesn't. You can put a blanket over it so you feel warm for a while, but the stress does not go away.

Maryann knows an energetic mom in her early thirties who spends about fifteen hours a week in the gym. If she were a gymnast training for the Olympics that might make sense, but a woman who has two young children, a full-time job and a marriage might want to ask herself why she feels the need to spend fifteen hours a week in the gym. Typically, we have a social bias *toward* this behavior. People around her admired her; she took their compliments and gave them advice: Working out increases your energy.

She had an addiction and it was starting to hurt her physically. The underlying issue was that she didn't feel a secure attachment to her husband, who ran a successful boutique software company. Her artificial attachment was working out all the time at the gym. She needed to use her relationship to calm down and not always run off to the gym.

Another case that drives home the point that addiction is about emotional need concerns a young woman addicted to shopping on television programs featuring infomercials and product deals. Her husband, who is a soldier, had multiple tours of duty abroad. When he was gone—and even when he was home, since he was emotionally unavailable to a great extent—she shopped. She got calls complimenting her on her taste and thanking her for being such a good customer. The callers would inquire, "Could we do anything else for you?" Desperate for a human connection, she kept shopping and they kept calling.

Finally, the credit card bills were more than the couple could handle. They divorced, with a judge shaking his head over the financial abuses perpetrated by the woman—a woman who had an artificial attachment when all she wanted was a secure attachment with her husband.

AUTHENTIC VULNERABILITY

Choosing to be vulnerable can open relationship opportunities the way opening a window can deliver fresh air to you. In its healthiest sense, vulnerability gives invigorating, cleansing, life-giving air to the person feeling it. In our society, though, it's all too common to see vulnerability as the open window that lets germs and fumes into your lungs.

At various points throughout this book, we have discussed the sad fact that our culture applauds toughness and wants us to barricade that window that might let in pollution and viruses. "Watch out for yourself!" is the pervasive message. The message of authentic vulnerability begins with the same words, but the impact is different: "Watch out for yourself by trusting that the people who care about you are watching out for you, too."

Choosing to be vulnerable is not something most people think is a good thing—at least in the United States. Almost everyone sees vulnerability as a profoundly negative state of being because of—what? It comes down to how we make fun of each other for the slightest transgressions and qualities. In chapter 4, we talked about the society-wide abuse of shame in pop culture. But we have absorbed that abuse to such a deep level in our relationships as well that even those we love are sometimes *afraid* of our judgment, *afraid* of what we think of them and how we will express our criticism. As Brené Brown said, "Shame is about disconnection. 'Is there something about me, if other people know it or see it, that I won't be worthy of connection?'"[1] She goes on to say that the only people who don't experience shame are those who have no capacity for empathy or human connection.

So feeling shame is normal, but trying to make sure we don't feel it is a significant way we prevent others from truly and deeply connecting with us. If we are to receive the health-sustaining and health-restoring benefits of intimate connections, we must remove the shame barrier and enter into vulnerability.

It's easier said than done. Whose life has been without shame and who hasn't, at some point, shamed another and injured the trust between them? Who has never been lied to, or experienced some kind of deception that betrayed trust? There is a litany of reasons why human beings have buckets of good excuses for not wanting to feel vulnerable. And yet, it is essential to making the connection so strong between two people that it can energetically help each be well and get well.

The way you know that you can begin to enjoy vulnerability with another person is by paying attention to signals from your body. The autonomic nervous system detects threats and the absence of threats. So you need to clue in to your physical experience of being with another person to determine whether or not you can move forward into a state of shared vulnerability. Start by pinpointing where you feel anxiety. Is it in the pit of your stomach? In your shoulders? Does your throat close up? When you aren't manifesting physical signs of anxiety, you're relaxed. Your body gives your brain distinct messages that you feel safe with a person.

SECURITY AND MIRACLE CURES

What if you received a diagnosis that you had a terminal illness—stage IV cancer, for example—but you had no fear about it? "That's not normal!" you're thinking, and we would agree with you. For some people, though, once their main criterion for security is met, they find the strength to face all kinds of things without any dread or panic. Speculate that for a person whose security is rooted in unconditional love, feeling that love makes her, on a day-to-day basis, a person living without fear. She trusts with her whole heart that her partner, children, friends and pets love her in an unqualified, enduring way.

It sounds like a great path to peace of mind, but is it enough for what some might call a "miracle cure?" There is science to back up an assertion that it *might*. We can start by taking a look at the reasons why cases like the following, reported by physicians in peer-reviewed journals, sometimes occur:

- A woman with spontaneous remission of acute adult T-cell leukemia/lymphoma[2]
- A man with spontaneous remission of lung cancer, described as "extensive metastatic disease"[3]
- Twelve cases of spontaneous regression of breast cancer[4]

The standard definition of spontaneous remission or spontaneous regression is that the disease no longer seems to pose a threat to the person, with the change occurring in the absence of adequate, accepted or conventional treatment. It's because the result does not nearly match the treatment that physicians say that they can't explain what happened; they can only speculate.

There are many possible explanations as to how spontaneous remission might occur, but the dominant one is that the person's immune system suddenly kicks into high gear. Another idea is that DNA methylation, which plays a role in giving cells their "job descriptions," could sometimes explain the change. As previous chapters have explored in depth, a person's emotional state—profoundly affected by his or her most intimate relationships—can have a pronounced effect on both the immune system and the DNA methylation process.

An article in *Discover* laid out a number of arguments for how the body affects spontaneous remissions in "The Body Can Beat Terminal Cancer—Sometimes." Opening with the profile of a man diagnosed with malignant melanoma and given eighteen months to

live, author Jeanne Lenzer then told about his dramatic, and seemingly inexplicable, victory over the deadly cancer.[5]

The man was John Matzke, happily married and a new dad
when the cancer struck him at the age of thirty. Before starting the
treatments, which he knew would be grueling, he took a few weeks
to build up his strength. During that month of hiking, meditating
and eating healthy, he developed something doctors call a halo sign
around the cancer site. It sounds like a heavenly occurrence, but it
is actually white rings that are evidence that the immune system is
attacking the cancerous cells.[6]

The intensity with which Matzke's immune system waged war
on his disease still seems mysterious, but Lenzer cites multiple sources
attesting to the vital role that the mind-body connection plays in both
triggering the immune system and in suppressing it. She also provides
an example of a remission that has been specifically linked to that
connection:

> *The scientific evidence that mind-body connections might
> induce self-healing is limited and conflicting. Nonetheless,
> some patients and physicians believe the mind plays a
> powerful role in both the development of cancer and its
> treatment. Alice Epstein, a mathematician and sociologist,
> was diagnosed in 1985 with cancer of the kidney and told
> that she should have her left kidney removed right away.
> One month after having her left kidney removed, the cancer
> spread to both her lungs, and she was informed she had just
> two to three months to live. Like Matzke, she was advised to
> undergo immediate treatment. Epstein, who says she had a
> 'cancer-prone personality,' then turned to psychosynthesis,
> which she describes as a 'combination of psychotherapy and
> spiritual therapy.' It helped her overcome depression, dif-
> ficulty expressing anger, and suppression of her own needs
> in order to please others—traits she and some psychologists
> believe are characteristic of the cancer-prone personality.
> Although she never received any medical or surgical*

treatment for the deadly cancer invading her lungs, six weeks
after starting psychosynthesis her tumors began to shrink.
Within one year, they had disappeared without a trace.[7]

When the article was published in September 2007, Epstein had been cancer-free for twenty-two years and was a healthy eighty-year-old.

Twelve years ago, Trevor's neighbor Florence was diagnosed with an aggressive cancer and given six months to live. She has a strong marriage and a tightly knit support network in her church. In fact, Trevor talked to members of this church and, when they got on the topic of what the most significant events were in the community in the past twenty years, one of the two things they said was, "When Florence got sick." It was as though they all heard the diagnosis and shared her disease—not in a negative way, but in a sense that it was their shared challenge to beat it.

Florence had ultimate faith in her secure relationships with her family and her church community. And she is truly healed.

CHAPTER 9

Practicing Radical Empathy
and Attunement

What does it mean to connect—to have your brain and another person's brain "share space" and to have your breathing and heartbeat match another person's? The implications for health and happiness are profound if you consider that, in an empathetic state, you actually feel someone else's pain or exhilaration. Your capacity for empathy means you feel as threatened as someone else even though you are perfectly safe.

Attunement is the driver of this kind of synchronicity. It allows you to be in a rhythmic place, a dance with another person. This underlies the dynamic expressed in the "Still Face" experiment and so many others involving the nature of relationships. The baby points, mom turns and looks to where the baby is pointing—it's a dance and you need to be listening, hearing and looking to the dance to experience attunement.

The story of Steve and Carly illustrates the opposite of attunement. Carly was feeling so distressed about the state of her marriage that she experienced extreme heart palpitations and had to be hospitalized. Rather than come to see her that evening, Steve went on a hike with his buddies. When asked about it, he said, "The doctor would have told me if it was a heart attack. It wasn't, so I went to the woods with my friends." Steve is not a sociopath, but this is a good example of sociopathic behavior: He could not emotionally tune in to his wife's feelings and needs. Sociopaths (clinically known as people with anti-social personality disorder) or psychopaths are not capable of connecting to another human being with attunement. They are not capable of empathy.

We commonly think of ourselves as sole individuals, but the reality is that others really do exist inside of us. It's a neurological event, that is, our brains actually operate as though "self" is composed of several interconnected people. We are not talking about the phenomenon of multiple personalities, nor are we being figurative.

The reason that we can experience empathy and attunement with other people is that our operating system is configured to make *learning to feel them* unavoidable unless we have something wrong with us. As suggested above, a condition that corrupts that operating system would be a serious anti-social personality disorder, such as psychopathy or sociopathy. People affected by such a disorder may see the social advantage of displaying empathy, but the process of learning to feel empathy and attunement is not supported by their brains.

A brief look at human physiology and discussion of brain imaging experiments provides information as to why we can feel each other's pain and just how intimate our neurological connections with other people can be. The nature of those connections is why we can say, in a literal sense, that relationships can tear down our health or help us heal and contribute to an ongoing state of well-being.

THE MECHANICS OF EMPATHY

Mirror neurons are the so-called roots of empathy and they are located behind our eyeballs. Neuroscientist Vilayanur Ramachandran started whipping up enthusiasm for the importance of mirror neurons in the early part of the twenty-first century and, to him, they represent all that makes us human.[1] They are the reason we feel pain when we go to the hospital and see a loved one with needles stuck in the veins of his hand. We can even feel it when we watch a movie with brutal killings. The sensation may be so intense that we have to look away. These motor neurons in mammalian brains physiologically give us the capacity for empathy.

It's important to focus on the concept of "capacity for empathy" in this discussion because, as of publication, the science is still divided on whether the presence of mirror neurons *causes* us to feel another person's emotions or whether their presence *enables* us to tune in to what a husband or pet or movie character is feeling. Do these neurons behind our eyeballs force us to be empathetic or do they make it possible for us to be empathetic?

Research done in the early 1990s pointed to an interesting phenomenon that led to the identification of mirror neurons. Giacomo Rizzolatti, an Italian researcher doing work with macaque monkeys, found that certain groups of neurons in the brain fired both when a monkey performed an action and when the monkey watched someone else do it. So even though these neurons belonged to the brain's motor system, they perked up in response to a goal or intention, not a specific movement.[2] Inspired by the discovery, a number of neuroscientists set out to determine if these mirror neurons were perhaps a missing link: If we can physiologically relate to someone else experiencing something as though we were experiencing it, then we have a scientific explanation for empathy.

The researchers went back to the laboratory to study how the mirror neuron system functions in both monkeys and humans. Published in 2004, their study, simply called "The Mirror-Neuron System," asserts that mirror neurons have two functions: to facilitate imitation and to help us understand the meaning of actions, that is, to help us turn perceived information into knowledge.[3]

Since much of what we learned about mirror neurons focused on that perceived information being visual, we wondered about blind people. What are their mirror neurons doing? The Italian researchers addressed this eloquently by noting that the subjects in the study showed that, as long as they received enough information through hearing, touch and/or description of an action to have a clear idea of what was happening, their mirror-neuron system was also active.[4]

The study also drew some distinctions between the capability of the monkeys' mirror-neuron systems and those of the human subjects. One is that the human systems code for movements forming an action and not strictly for action as the monkey mirror-neuron systems do. For example, you see or otherwise sense that the person who is crying in front of you is about to wipe her tears away; you don't have to wait for the action to happen to process that it will. The early signs are enough to trigger a response.

THE REQUIREMENTS FOR EMPATHY

Feeling empathy for another requires a couple of other experiential elements.

1. Compassion for self.
2. Not placing blame on the person with whom you want to have an empathetic connection.

In key ways, self-compassion is antithetical to self-esteem, which is an obsession of our culture.

Self-esteem is a comprehensive evaluation of self-worth, a determination of whether you are a good person or a bad person, a worthwhile person or a worthless person. In American culture, to have self-esteem you have to feel special and somehow above average. It's considered an insult to be average. If you're a woman and someone describes your looks as average, wouldn't you have the impulse to go buy some new makeup, get a new haircut or wear a pair of unique earrings? Reality check: Most people are average. Average looks, average intelligence, average accomplishments, average income. "Average" keeps the stores open, the government running and kids graduating from high school.

But we've sullied the concept. We give our children trophies for showing up. Kids swing the tee-ball bat until they get a hit. And then we applaud. We modify the grade structure so students can't fail, they can only receive a "remember to try harder" message and a pat on the back for not actually failing. Self-esteem is important for mental health; how we acquire it determines whether the impact on mental health is positive or negative.

This wayward approach to engendering self-esteem is a major factor in the growing epidemic of narcissism. It's a slippery slope: We start playing little games and manipulating facts to try and prop ourselves up while we put other people down. In short, we have a couple of generations of young people in which more and more of their members are full of themselves.

The definition of narcissism used by author Christopher Lasch, a historian at the University of Rochester who studied the problem in his classic work *The Culture of Narcissism*, expresses why narcissism is an airtight block to empathy. *The New York Times* explained it as follows:

"...the narcissist, driven by repressed rage and self-hatred, escapes into a grandiose self-conception, using other people as instruments of gratification even while craving their love and approval. Lasch saw the echo of such qualities in "the fascination with fame and celebrity, the fear of competition, the inability to suspend disbelief, the shallowness and transitory quality of personal relations, the horror of death."[5]

A practice that goes hand-in-hand with the cultural obsession with self-esteem is, oddly enough, self-criticism. We think we need self-criticism or we will be self-indulgent and lazy—and if that happens, we could end up *average*. In fact, self-criticism gets in the way of taking action that could genuinely build self-esteem. Self-criticism is self-injury; that is, we put ourselves under threat. The attack is not to our physical self, but to our self-concept. In chapter 3, we described the damage to the immune system that occurs when in a chronic state of fight-or-flight. A habit of self-criticism does exactly that. We are the attacker *and* the attacked. The process involves high levels of stress. In order to protect itself, the body shuts down to some degree. We feel depressed and have less energy. In short, if we use self-criticism to motivate ourselves to do better, we don't get what we want after all, because we're shut down!

Kristen Neff, associate professor of Human Development and Culture at the University of Texas at Austin, calls herself an evangelist for self-compassion. Neff points out that, in addition to our epidemic of narcissism, we also have a bullying epidemic. She links this to the obsession with self-esteem. Bullies build their self-esteem by being tougher and meaner than those around them. Another cultural problem she weaves into the discussion is prejudice, with people judging others as "less than" as a way of making themselves feel "more than."[6]

The opposite of all of these negative, self-esteem-related behaviors is self-compassion.

When we treat ourselves with patience and respect, when we show ourselves compassion, we reduce cortisol production and release feel-good hormones like oxytocin and opiates. We not only feel happier and more relaxed, but we have also made ourselves physically capable of having empathetic experiences with other human beings.

Blame puts a wedge between you and another person. This is really a corollary to the self-esteem discussion, since blame is another way one person puts him or herself above another person. It's also a corollary to the self-compassion discussion, since blame can also be self-directed; it's just one more way of a person attacking him or herself. Whether the blame is other-directed or self-directed, it shuts down the feel-good hormones and sends cortisol racing into the bloodstream as an automatic defense reaction.

When you are in a state of fight-or-flight, you don't become a "bad" person. You become a survivor—a self-absorbed, paranoid, opportunistic survivor. You don't have the parts of your brain that allow you to connect empathetically working at optimal levels. The fight-or-flight response moves you back into your reptilian brain, away from the mammalian and cognitive. Empathy requires that you be in touch with your own humanity.

THE EXPERIENCE OF EMPATHY

James A. Coan has done pioneering research in the neurological definition of "self" as well as the way the brain processes connections with other people. In chapter 6, we described his Hand Holding Experiment, which illustrates how one member of a couple has a reduction in perception of threat when the person's partner is holding his or her hand. Now we'll look at some of Coan's most recent followup research, which indicates dramatic discoveries in terms of empathy and attunement.

We know from brain imaging studies that certain regions of the brain are "threat responsive." The way those regions of the brain activate when self is under threat correlate tightly with the way they activate when a close friend is under threat. This doesn't tend to happen when a stranger is under stress, although we'll explain in a moment why it may. Coan notes:

> We think this is getting us close to the definition of what neural familiarity is. The self is flexible in terms of how the brain encodes what 'self' is. We think the whole idea of having a 'self' is a kind of conceptual white board that the brain uses for understanding other minds.
>
> A big thing that happens when we form a relationship with another person is that they become encoded as part of ourselves. That's part of the how the brain handles familiarity and closeness.[7]

Coan, we believe, is suggesting that all the old poetry and song lyrics about feeling like someone else is a part of us are true from a physiological perspective. So when we lose that person and say, "It's like I lost a part of myself!" that's more than a simile.

The brain uses an identifiable and describable process to understand alliances with other people. So becoming emotionally connected with another person is a physical event.

The first, most elementary thing that happens when you become familiar with someone is that you create a memory trace for that person via hippocampus and amygdala circuits. That happens with any kind of event; it gets physically encoded in your brain. But what happens with increased familiarity with a person? The person starts to become encoded as more than a memory: The individual gets encoded as "self" in other regions of the brain.

If we asked you to become self-conscious, we might begin by putting your focus on how you look, how you behave and how you speak. Using fMRI to view what your brain is doing in that state, we would see activity running along the midline of your brain. Researchers like Jim Coan see the same thing when they put people under "threat"—meaning that they do something that stimulates a fear response—because when people are under threat, they become very self-focused. The brain starts to do checks on various parts of the body, wondering, "Am I okay?"

When someone close to a person is threatened, researchers see the same kind of midline, prefrontal activity in their brain imaging. It's just as though the person's brain isn't distinguishing between "self" and "other."[8] Coan notes that even if researchers take measurements that are finely calibrated, they have a hard time telling the difference between a person's response under personal threat and the response to a partner or friend under threat.[9]

When Trevor's son was a little boy, he slipped on some rocks by the water once and she reached him and scooped him out of the water so quickly, she concluded that it was the fastest thing she'd ever done. There was no thinking involved. This is an extraordinarily efficient human response that probably every mother has experienced at least once. Coan links this response to the fact that Trevor's brain perceived that *she* was in danger and had an immediate response to that.[10] On a cognitive level, Trevor knew that it was her son, but her reaction bypassed that kind of mental processing. Thinking about how to take action would have delayed her moving to save the little boy. It's like the reason behind practicing for a sport: you want your responses to be automatic; you don't want thoughts to get in the way of your performance.

Visceral responses like Trevor's racing to save her son are always automatic. Your brain gets you to react quickly because you are bonded to the person. There is some gray area about this occurring with the protection of a strange child, and, of course, there are the stories of professionals like police officers and firefighters rapidly and heroically responding to save strangers. Generally, though, the brain would trigger this kind of lightning-quick emotional response with someone who is close to you.

When this phenomenon occurs, one of the things that is going on is understanding the other person's state. In the case of Trevor's child, she had to have a good sense of what was happening to him. On some level, her brain was tricked into thinking it was happening to her. There was, in a real sense, no distinction between mother and son, so Trevor reacted automatically on behalf of him as though she was the one who had fallen into the water.

One day, when Maryann was living in Washington, DC, she saw a little girl running and jumping on some steps outside a townhouse. The girl missed her footing and started falling head first toward the cement pavement. Maryann barely knew this child, but she dove underneath her, placing her hands under the child's head. Years later, she still has small scars on her hands from that incident. Coan explains that saving a stranger like that child says something about the adult's family of origin. It is the kind of empathetic reaction associated with someone who grew up in a loving home where people cared for and protected each other. In contrast, this is likely not the automatic emotional response from someone who grew up in harsh circumstances.[11]

EXPLORING ATTUNEMENT

Feeling compassion for ourselves is the gateway emotion to our connecting energetically with other people. In an episode of the original *Star Trek* television series, an "empath" is the central character in torture experiments conducted on key members of the Enterprise crew. Her ability to connect with other beings on an empathetic level is so strong that her energy can heal them.[12] Unfortunately, the more healing she has to do, the weaker she gets, until her own life is at risk. This may be the nature of empathy on her planet, but on planet Earth we humans need to feel compassion and love for ourselves first before we can connect openly and generously with another. We humans actually get stronger, not weaker, from empathizing.

Energetic connection may sound like a metaphysical concept until we look at the work of someone like Paul Ekman, a pioneer in the study of emotions and their relation to facial expressions. We are hard-wired to recognize certain emotions in other human beings, regardless of their facial structure or specific features. We recognize disgust, anger, happiness, sadness, fear and surprise in each other.[13] That leads to an important follow-up question: What else do we sense about each other, and how do we sense it?

When we look closely at how people detect each other's emotions, we see that Ekman was right—with a caveat. We do have universal recognition of certain emotions due to the way our faces express them, but it seems we get true understanding of strong emotions only by watching the rest of the body as well. So, while it's valid to make statements about the face-heart connection, recent research indicates we might want to expand that concept to the body-heart connection. Hillel Aviezer led a multinational team of psychologists conducting experiments that resulted in the report "Body Cues, Not Facial Expressions, Discriminate Between Intense Positive and Negative Emotions."[14]

People participating in the study looked at only the faces of tennis players at critical moments of play, then the bodies with the faces erased, then the faces plus the bodies. The subjects could not determine the emotion of the players based on faces alone. They correctly identified the emotions based on body alone, and they had the same success when they saw face and body combined.[15]

Then Aviezer added a twist just to be sure of what his team was finding. He manipulated the photographs, putting faces of winners on the bodies of losers and vice versa. The results belie what we've thought for years. Aviezer found that the same facial expression was interpreted completely differently based on what the body was doing. People in the study were certain that the clues they got about the emotion came from information contained in the face, like narrowed eyes or pursed lips. Those clues were not valid, though.[16]

In chapter 8 we discussed Danny, whose face showed an emotional transformation after his wife expressed unqualified appreciation for the way he cared for their children. That is true but perhaps a better way to link that experience to attunement is to recognize that his sudden feeling of security permeated his body, essentially inviting his wife to a "dance of trust." When they hugged, they had a harmonious connection from head to toe.

THE LANGUAGE OF ATTUNEMENT

We want to begin teaching you a foreign language that will help you improve your relationships and your health. Trevor asks every couple that comes in for counseling to learn this foreign language—the language of attunement. In a way, this manner of expressing emotion is the opposite of medical language, which employs terms such as "paroxysmal supraventricular tachycardia." Couples often come in thinking they should aim for that kind of specificity in talking about their lives and emotions. To carry the analogy further, what they need to learn to say is "occasional rapid heart rate," not "paroxysmal supraventricular tachycardia." After that, they need to make it even more personal: "sometimes my heart throbs like someone just pulled a gun on me."

John Gottman, co-founder with his wife of The Gottman Relationship Institute, is an award-winning psychologist who is known globally for his work on marital stability and divorce. He expressed his frustration with the language of his own profession in terms of talking about human behavior and emotion in a 1995 paper. In discussing his own descriptions of marital interaction, he said:

> *I did not want my summary codes to read something like: 'Husband shows zygomatic major contracts on face with contraction of the cheek raiser muscle, with shift downward in fundamental frequency, decrease in amplitude and voice in a major key and rapid inhalation and exhalation of breath with hut hut vocalizations.' Instead, I wanted to say that the husband laughed.*[17]

The work he did with James Coan (referenced in chapter 3) for his Hand Holding Experiment resulted in The Specific Affect Coding System (SPAFF), which serves as a very useful guide for those of us in clinical practice in identifying certain emotion-based behaviors in a couple, then helping the couple recognize those behaviors themselves, and then finally giving voice to their understanding of the emotions they're feeling and trying to express.[18]

A key premise of SPAFF is that people express their emotions in myriad ways, so watertight definitions of what trust or disdain sound like or look like have no place in this system. It helps clinicians connect the signs displayed by a person, or a couple, with emotional behaviors as follows: neutral, humor, affection/caring, interest/curiosity, surprise, validation, anger, disgust/scorn, contempt, whining, sadness, fear, belligerence, dominance, stonewalling and defensiveness.

Clinicians using SPAFF pay attention to verbal content, facial behaviors, voice tones and other methods of communication. To further explain what we mean by "the language of attunement," right now we're just going to focus on the vocal elements.

When one partner speaks the language of attunement in expressing affection to the other, he conveys genuine caring and concern very clearly. His partner feels comforted and has no doubt that "you have my back!" The pace of communication may slow down a bit and the tone of voice generally gets quieter. The voice of affection is a soothing voice which invites bonding. In their chapter on SPAFF in the *Handbook of Emotion Elicitation and Assessment*, Coan and Gottman cite the following verbal cues as indicators of affection:[19]

- *Reminiscing.* One partner shares warm memories of something she and her partner enjoyed together.
- *Caring statements.* These are direct statements of affection or concern, such as "I love you," "I care about you," "I worry about you" and similar expressions.
- *Compliments.* One partner makes statements that convey pride in or admiration of the other partner, for example, "You handled that so well!"
- *Empathy.* Verbal mirroring often expresses empathy. It's easy to hear that one partner is tuned into her partner's feelings, and that those feelings have a deep level of significance to her.
- *Common cause.* Sometimes this is known as the common enemy. It's an indication that the couple is standing shoulder-to-shoulder on an issue and shows a desire to bond and agree. What comes out of the mouth may not sound affectionate since it may be both parties calling her boss a jerk, but the clear message is that they share that opinion of the boss.
- *Flirting.* When partners flirt, they communicate desire for each other. Flirting can be playful, sweet, warm, intense or all of the above.[20]

You are not abnormal if using language in the ways just discussed seems foreign or contrived. In this culture, men are particularly distanced from the language of attunement. Trevor went to a lecture given by Diana Fosha, founder of Accelerated Experiential-Dynamic Psychotherapy (AEDP), and as part of it, Fosha shared a case study that was partially presented through videotaped sessions. A young man had seen his girlfriend flirting with someone, so he went into another room and destroyed a chair. His girlfriend told him that she would break up with him if he didn't go into therapy. He struggled with conversations centered on emotions and often looked as though he were about to cry, but he forced his face into neutral expressions as he held in the tears. The therapist observed that the young man looked sad. To that he replied, "I don't use the word 'sad.'"

His backstory was that he was achievement based all his life, with siblings who received most of the parental attention. He had not had anyone to help him walk through his emotions. He'd had no coaching in expressing how he felt.

The therapist asked him if he felt safe with him. Again, the young man seemed disconnected from the concept. He wasn't in touch with any experience of people caring whether or not he felt safe with them, much less actually asking him whether or not he felt safe. To him, he might question his sense of safety if he were about to get into a bar fight, not when he was sitting in a room with some guy doing psychotherapy.

In another session, the therapist commented that he'd thought about the young man during the week, was concerned about him and hoped that things were going okay. It's important to let clients know that they exist in your world and are important to you. Nevertheless, we—that is, almost anyone in this society—are not accustomed to drawing a man into that kind of soft, caring conversation.

Our society finds it to be generally acceptable to make a joke at another's expense (more on that in a minute), but we have not given young men the toolkit to communicate a simple emotional concept like "sad" or "safe." Even listening to the language of attunement can be an alien experience.

Given that we believe there is such a thing as the language of attunement, it's not a stretch to conclude we also believe there's an anti-attunement language. One perfect example is something we consider so acceptable that it's an integral part of our entertainment culture: mean-spirited humor. Put-down humor exacerbates the defense mechanisms we employ so that we don't appear vulnerable, so it's very consistent with the American lone-cowboy mentality. This style of humor is a pervasive and, unfortunately, effective way of regulating intimacy.

A young couple with a one-year-old child suffered greatly from this kind of humor. John was a very handsome, well-groomed lawyer. Jill had physical beauty, but she gained a lot of weight during her pregnancy and kept much of it on. In the course of a session, when talking about something unrelated, John found ways of stuffing zingers related to Jill's appearance into the conversation. He'd say things like, "We did enjoy going to that event together. By the way, didn't your friend Janet look great in that brown dress? You'd look like a sausage in it!" Jill's friend Janet had a baby the same month she did, but Janet lost the weight she had gained during pregnancy. Anyone could have seen the sense of embarrassment and humiliation in Jill's face when John made the sausage "joke." John had to deflect attention from her look of dejection, so he made another "joke."

Any sensitive person's initial reaction would be horror, but John wasn't actually a mean person who wanted to make his wife miserable. This kind of humor had simply become part of his coping style. His father had died of alcoholism while John was in law school. So here was a highly functional and academically successful young man whose father was found dead in a gutter outside the local bar.

He used mean humor to keep his own feelings from wounding him in tender places. He didn't want to deal with the sadness and loss of his father, so anytime he had an encounter that might make him feel vulnerable, he said something sarcastic or mean with the veneer of wit.

If John did this at home, you can be certain he also did it at work and probably at the gym, his place of worship and everywhere else he went. In *The First-Time Manager*, author Jim McCormick gives sound advice on this from a business perspective. He cautions, "Avoid expense humor, meaning humor of any kind that is at another person's expense. Doing otherwise will make you look petty and insecure."[21]

Oddly enough, put-down humor is generally socially acceptable, but it can severely damage personal relationships of any kind if the other person hears the meanness and not the humor. If you grow up with a father who makes jokes and puts you down, what does that do to your immune system? If you're married to a woman who never misses a chance to mock your choice of shirt or your haircut, what does that do to your immune system? If you have a boss who uses sarcasm to make himself look clever while you look foolish, what does that do to your immune system? If you have a child who brings his "cool" humor home and makes fun of your cooking and taste in furniture, what does that do to your immune system? Consider that this kind of humor is potentially a form of abuse—and, if so, causes inflammation the way other forms of abuse do.

Put-down humor primes the target of the joke to have a shift in self-perception. The social justification is "she'll get over it" and "it wouldn't be funny if there wasn't some truth in it"—as though spotlighting the fact that someone looks fat in a dress is a truth the world needs to focus on. Advertisers have intimate familiarity with the concept of priming, and those behind negative campaign ads are priming geniuses.

As much as candidates and their supporters may protest negative campaign ads as "dirty" or "undignified," they work. The reason they work provides a caution to all of us regarding the negative messages we send through put-down humor, harsh criticism of partners and co-workers, and so on. At the risk of somewhat oversimplifying the conclusions of political scientists, the reasons boil down to the facts that negative ads are perceived as having relevant information, viewers/listeners give greater weight to negative versus positive information and negative ads evoke stronger emotional responses.[22] We are not suggesting we run around uttering "peace and love!" and spritzing each other with lavender mist. We're saying that our society would not engender disease to the extent it currently does if the content and tone of our language rose to a more positive level.

Among the most famous put-downs are those involving stereo-
types. Even in an age of political correctness, they thrive. (Now please
silence the little voice in your head that says they thrive because they
contain a kernel of truth.) Margaret Shih, Todd L. Pittinsky and Nalini
Ambady of the department of Psychology at Harvard University did a
priming study with Asian women as part of their work on stereotype
susceptibility. It shows how easy—and effective—it can be to shift a
person's self-perception, and as a result, the person's performance.[23]
Prior to taking a mathematics test, all of the women completed a questionnaire about residential life at their university. But there were actually two different questionnaires: One emphasized gender-related
issues and the other, ethnicity. In American society, both "woman"
and "Asian" have a stereotypical association with math. Women are
bad at it and Asians are good at it. There was no reason in terms of intelligence and prior academic history that would indicate why some of
the Asian women would do much better on the math test than others.
In fact, participants in the study all had excellent quantitative skills
as evidenced by their SAT scores. Yet the research team found the
following: "Participants in the Asian identity salient condition performed significantly better than participants in the female identity
salient condition."[24]

We were struck by the phrase "significantly better" in their conclusion. It's a compelling statement about the power that language
has to influence how we feel about ourselves and relate to our environment. In *Locus of Control*, psychologist Herbert Lefcourt, whose
legacy primarily relates to laughter being the best medicine, describes a heartbreaking situation that illustrates how much words can
hurt. Denise, a woman who had been institutionalized for a decade,
was among the patients moved to a different floor while the hospital
was undergoing renovations. Up to that point, Denise had been kept
in a section of the hospital that people in the facility talked about
as the "chronic/hopeless" area. Before moving the patients there to
the new floor, the staff gave everyone thorough exams. Denise, even

though she never spoke and was very withdrawn, seemed to be in excellent health. After moving to the new floor, which housed patients who were a step away from discharge, she started talking to people and interacting with staff and other patients. When renovations were complete, patients from the "chronic/hopeless" floor moved back into their rooms. Within a week, Denise died. An autopsy did not point to any medical cause for her death.[25] One possible answer was described in chapter 1—broken heart syndrome. Clearly, there's a flaw in the logic of "sticks and stones can break my bones, but words can never hurt me." We don't mean to suggest that it was the words alone that changed her health situation by breaking her heart, but the symbolic power of labeling human beings "hopeless" cannot be overestimated, either.

Taking into account that couples tend to seek counseling about seven years after they first experience marital problems, can you imagine how many couples coming in for their first session with Trevor talk about their relationship with words like "hopeless"? The next thing they usually do is tell her how it got that way, namely, it's the "he did this/she did that" conversation. They speak almost nothing but the language of anti-attunement until they understand that it's not sticks and stones that are breaking their hearts. We hope that, after reading this book, you understand that the way you communicate with others can quickly build trust and a sense of security—or shred them just as quickly.

In her book *Counterclockwise: Mindful Health and the Power of Possibility*, psychologist Ellen Langer succinctly explains both the utility and the shortcomings of language. Her take on it gives depth to the concept of "the language of attunement," which involves the way people express a mutually-felt sense.

> *When you ask me how I feel and I tell you I have a stomachache, I presume that your experience of stomachaches enables you to understand that I feel reasonably unwell. But the many possible differences between our experiences*

get lost, as language creates an illusion of knowing.
Language is shorthand; individual experience is the full
text.[26]

The language of attunement is a giant step away from what language usually is, that is, a tool for communicating a single perspective. When you talk about how your stomach hurts, you aren't trying to understand what someone else feels like when her stomach hurts. In contrast, the language of attunement is a tool of empathy. It is a way of communicating that is as much about listening as it is about talking. It is about trying to use words to energize the heart connection between you and another person.

Langer cites the value of introducing conditional language into conversations about health as a way of opening our minds to possibilities rather than resigning ourselves to certainties. First, we'll explain the concept and then we suggest that you try an exercise around conditional words to help develop more proficiency in the language of attunement.

When a medical doctor delivers a diagnosis and then a prognosis related to your recovery after discovering a growth in your breast, it might go something like this: "The biopsy indicates that you have breast cancer; however, since we detected it early, we will get you into surgery promptly. With chemotherapy and radiation, we remain optimistic about your chances for survival." What you are likely to hear from his words: "You have cancer. We are going to operate and then pump you full of drugs and shoot you with rays. After that, if you're lucky, you'll live." Langer proposes an alternative way of speaking that shifts the patient's perception of her situation: "Imagine an approach that opens us up to uncertainty, which opens us up to possibility."[27] She offers phrases such as "in my view" as a way for a physician to qualify a diagnosis—realizing, of course, that many people will argue that the doctor ought to sound certain or he or she loses credibility.

But consider this: Objective, absolute language suggests a single reality, whereas the addition of conditional words and phrases implants the reality that we have choices and can, in fact, explore possibilities. Langer's research showed that introducing conditional words such as "could be" or "perhaps" led to patients' thinking about their diagnoses in different ways. They asked questions. They were co-participants in a discussion rather than victims of a medical verdict. In other words, this isn't about positive thinking; it's about possibility thinking.[28]

Let's apply this approach to a personal relationship. A common combination of anxious pursuer and avoidantly attached person are having a dialogue about getting their older son ready for his imminent move to a college dorm. The anxious pursuer, who has a near obsession with problem solving, is using a lot of phrases like "we should" and "we have to" in relation to preparations for the young man to leave. The avoidant one half-listens. He expects his anxious pursuer partner to talk like that so tuning out is, to him, acceptable. In online marketing terms, the anxious pursuer would be using push communication; the avoidant partner is essentially hitting the delete button when it comes in. In moving toward the language of attunement, the anxious pursuer would make some minor adjustments such as "We should *probably* find out…" and "We *may* have to…" Following that conditioned statement with a question like "What do you think?" is a small move—albeit an important one—toward the language of attunement.

Attunement Exercise

Now that you hopefully have a sense of your attachment style, use that knowledge in reaching out through language to your partner and/or to other people in your life with whom you have intimate relationships. The next time you have a conversation in which imperatives could be involved ("We should" or "We have to"), whether you are the one inclined to issue the orders or hear them, step back and then:

- If you are the one inclined to give the plan of action, modify it with a conditional. For example, "We could…what do you think?"
- If you are the one on the receiving end of the action plan, respond with a possibility. For example, "Sure, that could work. Just wondering what you thought of this…"

We won't try to delude you. This may not yield any immediate breakthroughs. Try it, though. Repeatedly. You may be surprised about the new "possibility conversations" that will flow from it.

THE BODY LANGUAGE OF ATTUNEMENT

Here we're going to deviate from the SPAFF, which says that there are no particular "action units," that is, physical cues, that indicate affection. Earlier in this chapter, we discussed Aviezer's study regarding the ability to read emotions based on what the body is doing, regardless of what the face is doing. We're going to take that approach here, drawing from the extensive body-language research and instruction done by Gregory Hartley, co-author with Maryann of seven books on human behavior.

In *I Can Read You Like a Book*, Hartley and Maryann took a holistic approach to reading a person's mood that was quite consistent with what Coan and Gottman said in the SPAFF description when they referenced hard-to-describe, yet critical, indicators such as "positive energy."[29] They combined understanding movements with the elements of energy, direction and focus. These criteria would be classed as follows:

> **Energy**: high or low
> **Direction**: sharp or scattered
> **Focus**: internal, external or stimulus dependent[30]

Based on that system, we would summarize a description of the body language of attunement by saying that it is high energy, sharp direction, with an external focus. These features are combined with movements indicating openness; these are movements that convey a desire to connect.

High energy does not imply jumping up and down on Oprah Winfrey's couch, as movie star Tom Cruise infamously did in declaring his love for Katie Holmes. In this context, it refers to energy flowing head to toe that projects a sense of life and well-being. Although he can move very little of his body anymore due to motor neuron disease, the renowned theoretical physicist Stephen Hawking has a high-energy demeanor.

Sharp direction suggests moving toward a goal. Two people who want to experience attunement have the common goal of being part of each other, feeling the same rhythm of emotions as well as the same physical rhythms of their heartbeats and breathing.

Someone with internal focus would be confused, distracted or perhaps contemplative. None of those moods describe a person actively engaged in developing attunement. External focus in this context, then, is other-focused. It is a state of paying attention to a partner.

Movements of openness are relative to a specific person when it comes to attunement. Someone who strides jauntily down the street with his arms swinging exhibits openness. Someone sitting at a conference table with her laptop closed during a meeting exhibits openness. But neither of these people has open body language with the purpose of achieving attunement with a particular individual.

In the context of a relationship, openness means angling the body toward your partner and leaning in. It means eliminating the barriers between you and your partner, whether they are body parts like arms or inanimate objects like pillows. Open body language can also relate to clothing. If you and your partner are sitting in session with Trevor and the aim is to engender a sense of attunement, then wearing a stiffly starched (translate: untouchable) outfit is not the "fashion of attunement."

One of Trevor's clients recently told her husband in a session, "I can tell when you emotionally vacate." What she then described was the opposite of the body language of attunement. He would move in the direction of "still face" and angle his body away from her slightly. This is using the body as a barrier and, even though it may be subtle, it sends the same message as if he had suddenly taken out his cell phone and started texting—an act that some people feel is appropriate in any circumstance.

This example of anti-attunement body language points to a problem that is society-wide. Without any awareness of how they are undermining their relationships, many people physically put gadgets between them and their loved ones on a regular basis. We remember being told, "Look at me when I talk to you!" when we were growing up. The importance of that message is that eye contact engages one of our senses in the connection. It removes the barrier of a magazine or a gadget and establishes an uncluttered, face-to-face relationship.

We encourage you to do two things in getting yourself acquainted with the body language of attunement. At least once a day, look your partner in the eyes. The contact can be brief, but do it deliberately and send the message, "I'm glad to see you." Raise your awareness of barriers between you and your partner when you're talking to that person—cell phone, kitchen counter, crossed arms and so on. Consciously get rid of the barriers. What you are communicating is an invitation to share space and the message that you feel safe with that person.

LIVING IN CONNECTION

We are hard-wired to care about each other. This is where Charles Darwin loses credibility. Other creatures, humans and the non-human mammals who share our households, understand the pain we feel on some level. A "dog-eat-dog" mentality is not normal or natural for human beings.

The restorative power of living in connection must be respected. It's vital that you show up for people, let them show up for you and take a stand on relationships whenever possible. The alternative is undermining our ability to have relationships by disposing of them when they don't work, avoiding problems and/or pathologizing difficult issues so we have an excuse to medicate the pain away.

Discussions of our over-medicated society tend to lay blame on the professionals who prescribe the drugs and the companies that make them. We think we're missing a key piece of information about the problem, which is that medication attacks a health issue on an individual level and some of the health issues being attacked are actually relational problems. The conditions may be muted or improved by a pill, but they won't be fixed. Trevor has couples come in, ostensibly ready to move to a new level of intimacy with their relationship, and they are on so many anti-anxiety and anti-depressant medications that she's surprised they know each others' names. That approach to coping is starting earlier and earlier in people's lives. Millennials are not only the most stressed-out generation, according to the American Psychological Association; they are also the most needlessly medicated.[31] We've inadvertently trained our children to enhance their medical vocabulary so they can describe maladies to doctors that will get them the drugs they want. At the same time, we haven't helped them cultivate a vocabulary of relationships.

Here is an example of what we mean about a situation that requires connection and would likely be exacerbated with medication. Trevor's friend's husband suffers from cancer. At times, he does remarkably well; other times, he fades and falters, relying tremendously on his wife's caregiving. When his condition deteriorated substantially and the demands on her were constant, she e-mailed her eight closest friends and said, "I am really angry. I'm really depressed. I am so frustrated. I need to meet with all of you. Are you available Thursday night? I'll be at [a local restaurant] at eight P.M. Whoever can come, please show up." They all came.

She laid out her feelings and circumstances. No holding back. The women plunged deeply into the world of someone who spent her days and nights caring for a cancer patient undergoing nightmarish treatments. Normally, this is a group that does not go down such a path, instead keeping up appearances and staying on a very friendly, but polite, plane.

Two of the women immediately jumped in and said, "You really should take medication." They offered the phone numbers of their doctors and made the case for how much better she would feel in a couple of weeks if she would just start taking anti-depressants. One even said, "I started on them ten years ago. You'd be surprised what you can get through with the help of a little dose of meds."

"With all due respect, no." Trevor said. "This is life. There are hard parts of life. You're feeling things that you need to feel right now. You don't get to be in this fully if you medicate your feelings away. It's appropriate for you to feel this way and your reaching out to us and bringing your friends closer to you is exactly how you can get through this. Without meds."

Afterward, Trevor discussed this case with psychiatrist David M. Reiss, well known for his work in character and personality dynamics. Here are his thoughts:

> *Frustration, disappointment, sadness and grief are*
> *uncomfortable but normal aspects of life. Prescription of*
> *anti-depressant medication to suppress what are actually*
> *healthy, even if uncomfortable, emotional reactions is*
> *counter-productive, instilling a sense of helplessness and*
> *victimization as opposed to encouraging a mature under-*
> *standing of the vicissitudes of life, toleration of discomfort*
> *and how to appropriately seek comforting from safe and*
> *reliable personal relationships—intimate, family, friends,*
> *spiritual and so on.*[32]

Trevor's friend is a strong woman and a connected person. Her life did not get easier for a while, but she eventually made it through—with help from her friends and no "help" from her friends' doctors. In the previous chapter, we described how "miracle cures" can happen. There will be no shortage of these miracles if we truly show up for each other like that.

When we consider how dramatically a secure connection can affect well-being, we invariably think of one of our favorite stories about members of Trevor's immediate family.

Trevor's sister Michon spent months in the hospital with her son, Hib, who had acute myeloid leukemia, a rare form of pediatric cancer that required such drastic chemotherapy that he had to be hospitalized for six months. Throughout that time, Michon slept on a cushion tucked near a window, not able to stretch out.

Hib's immune system was severely compromised, so the world around him was a threat to him. Hib was like the title character in the movie *Bubble Boy* who couldn't risk exposure to an environment full of germs and had to live in a protective sphere.

Michon knew everything about the care of her son. If the medication was fifteen minutes late, for example, she knew it. She was on top of every aspect of his treatment. Most important, she was by his side giving him love and joy.

One night at around 2 A.M., Michon grew concerned by Hib's high fever and other dire symptoms. She knew something was wrong. Alerting a resident, she explained that something needed to be done immediately. However, the resident concluded it was fine to wait until morning. Michon pushed back: "No," she said. "Notify his attending physician now."

That got no response, so she asked the nurse on duty to alert the doctor, who arrived promptly. He suspected an infected PICC (peripherally inserted central catheter). This is a slender tube that goes into the arm and terminates in a large vessel near the heart. As soon as test results came back confirming his suspicions, he immediately removed the PICC line. Hib would likely have died without Michon's intervention.

Next door to Hib, there was a little girl whose parents never showed up. She whimpered all night long—in pain and lonely. It is a story of suffering with a sad conclusion. One day, she was wheeled off to the ICU and never returned.

In contrast, Hib's story had a happy ending. Michon's investment in every tiny detail of how her son was doing paid off. No single nurse or doctor had such a moment-by-moment knowledge of his condition. Her connection to him remained strong and resilient; love trumped inconvenience.

Hib is thriving. He will graduate from college in the spring of 2014, has a wonderful girlfriend and treasures the connections that kept him alive.

Living in connection is certainly about relationships; however, as we've discussed throughout this book, relationships are part of a system that sustains and restores health. Daniel Siegel calls this system the "triangle of well-being" and he describes it as three interdependent elements that cannot be reduced to any fewer. The loss of any one jeopardizes human health; conversely, the presence of all three supports human health.[33]

The first part is relationships. When your most important relationships—with your partner, a child, a parent and so on—are jeopardized, your mental health is jeopardized. The second part is the brain, the mechanism that sends information throughout the entire body—information about relationships and environmental factors that influence the body. It needs to function well to contribute to the strength of the triangle. The third is the mind, defined earlier in this book as a process, without which information cannot be shared between two people and without which the body itself is not properly informed about what's going on in the brain.[34]

A key point is that the mind is not merely the activity of the brain; in fact, Siegel said, "That makes no sense. We know the mind can actually change the structure of the brain, just like the brain influences the mind."[35] The legs of the triangle are truly interdependent.

Siegel's climactic statement about the nature of the "triangle of well-being" captures a central tenet of this book:

> *You can use the flow of energy information from your rela-*
> *tionship to alter the way synapses fire off in the brain.*
> *And we now know from studies of neuroplasticity that you*
> *can promote the growth of the brain structure itself by*
> *experiences and relationships.*[36]

Returning to the discussion of the deep cellular and multi-generational effects of our relationships and other environmental factors, Siegel adds:

> *Experience in relationships actually changes the regula-*
> *tion of the genes in the neurons of the skull-based brain.*
> *So relationships are not just some casual "wouldn't that be*
> *nice, we're all from California, we like to love each other"*
> *thing, relationships are actually what the brain requires for*
> *healthy growth.*[37]

We've offered you labels for concepts that relate to the act of living in connection. From Siegel's "triangle of well-being" to Trevor's "couples coding" and "language of attunement," these phrases are meant to help you organize your thoughts around the *possibilities* for your relationships. They are meant to give you ideas about how to be so deeply, energetically connected to another person that you have the power to transform each other's health and well-being.

As we've said so many times in so many ways, though, applying concepts like these is not transformational if all that you are doing is thinking about them. The healing power of relationships comes from the healing power of emotions. So let the concepts help you organize your thoughts, and then put your heart into them.

Conclusion

Most people like being right. It's one of the characteristics we share that has a good side and a bad side. The bad side is that we sometimes stand our ground, even about petty things. The good side is that we dig and dig in an effort to unearth the facts of the matter or the proof of the assertion. This book took you skimming across an ocean of evidence that loving relationships can literally save your life.

In *Forging Healthy Connections*, we've offered scientific proof that your entire body responds to relationships, positively and negatively. And it isn't just your own body that's affected by relationships if you're a mother: Your stress and your nurturing potentially affect the health and well-being of multiple generations.

Emotions have great healing power; they also have the power to make you sick—really sick. The notion that you can "change your mind" or "focus your thoughts" to be healthy or reverse an illness is flawed. You need to engage your emotions, too. Your thoughts are like unarmed warriors on the battlefield without the power of your emotions.

Because intimate connections to other people are a full-bodied experience (whether they are friendships, love affairs, mentoring relationships, family ties or anything else), their importance in your life is unmistakable. You will support both your health and your healing by ascertaining the quality of those relationships. We've tried to help you do that in a supportive way, a way that does not involve judgment of yourself or others for not being a "perfect" spouse, parent or friend. Rather, we want you to see the joy in feeling compassion for yourself and others, regardless of the flaws.

A big part of the discussion is how incredibly destructive chronic stress is. It perpetuates a high-alert state that can badly damage your immune system. Recently, a senior executive under extraordinary daily pressure, including trying to finish the manuscript for a new book, asked Maryann how to mitigate the stress she was feeling. She and Maryann had talked about the effects of stress on health. "When you go home tonight, go straight to your husband and let him hug you," Maryann said. "When we talk next, tell me how you felt." The executive later said, "I felt like I was melting. My world seemed softer. And then I lay down on the couch, put my head on a pillow and dozed off." Clearly, the stress was gone, at least for awhile.

We wondered if there is something terribly wrong with our society that creates disadvantages for people in terms of relationships. In other words, do we live in a culture that actually sabotages our relationships and therefore our health? The unfortunate answer is, "Yes." Because of what we hear, read and see, it's terribly easy to have mismatches between expectations and reality, and then to get impatient or dismissive with potentially good relationships because the reality of them doesn't meet our fantastical expectations. It's consistent with our culture to romanticize the loner, the cowboy and the rogue, even though they represent lack of connection and an insular existence that's essentially unhealthy.

But we offer hope. Lately the value and necessity of connections and how our society needs to embrace them a bit better has become news. The moving and authentic ways that Bostonians responded to the Boston Marathon bombing illustrated that reaction perfectly.

We also offer hope about your ability to forge healthy connections, regardless of your previous experiences. You can change—not just because you decide to, but because it feels good.

The tough work we have ahead as a society is to make it possible for all of us to have vibrant, secure relationships. This is a societal issue, and the reasons supporting that assertion are sprinkled throughout this book. Now here is one more reason, embodied in a quote made famous by then First Lady of the United States Hillary Rodham Clinton in her bestseller, *It Takes a Village*: "It takes a village to raise a child." The premise is that all of the people in a caregiving role, as well as those who have significant influence over a child's development, impact that child's well-being.

What if the village had asked more questions about Adam Lanza, the young man who massacred twenty schoolchildren in Newtown, Connecticut? What if, as a society and as individuals, we try to reach out and include those fragile few who are so dissociated, so unfeeling, so devalued, that they feel they have to kill to get in touch with other human beings?

The neurological pathways we groove into our children from the time they are born either prepare them for loving relationships or make it hard for them to cultivate those relationships. When we look for causes of epidemics of mental and physical illnesses, we need to weave "quality of relationships" into the discussion. The generation we call Millennials, now in their twenties, has been officially declared "the most stressed out," according to the American Psychological Association. Sure, we blame individual parents for not helping their kids develop coping skills or genuine self-esteem, but a problem that widespread also reflects systemic issues in society. Somehow, we failed to nurture their appreciation for the kinds of connections that would, in fact, de-stress them. Somehow, we failed to engender an appreciation for co-regulation.

Another aspect of the "it takes a village" premise is what our society needs to do to support parents who must work. As Trevor told her daughter when she expressed a desire to "take a few years off to raise children," most people can't afford that anymore. Unless an advanced race of benevolent aliens teaches us how to propagate the prosperity of the "one percent," her daughter will not be staying home and she will need to find daycare like most other mothers. Whoever provides that daycare contributes to the pathways that either give them relationship advantages or struggles.

As a corollary, by not addressing the dire need for widespread quality childcare and early learning opportunities, we are ignoring the lessons of epigenetics. We aren't "grooming the rat pups;" therefore, those rat pups will turn out to be lousy parents and lousy citizens— not because of their genes, but because we didn't bother to groom them. They will practice negligence and pass those negligent practices on to the next generation. This is the underlying logic for our assertion that deficiencies in social welfare programs and lack of educational opportunities foster impoverished communities.

But we don't want to end with a sharp warning and a prayer for alien intervention. We want to turn to the good news about what transformational things are possible right now, regardless of the societal and family mistakes of the past.

Our brains are plastic, meaning that they can be re-shaped in a neurobiological sense. We do not have to repeat the misery of feeling disconnected or rejected as a child or as an adult. We have the possibility of proactively re-grooving our neurological pathways. We start by acknowledging who and what has hurt us—who and what has put us into a state of fight-or-flight—and then find the company of people who take us into their hearts and enable us to feel safe.

When you lean in to your partner or a dear friend and seek comfort and compassion, you open yourself to a thrilling combination of serenity and excitement. It is the energy of health and healing. Throughout your life, continue to call on it and keep connected.

Afterword and Acknowledgements

In my world, Ellen Langer is significant for two reasons: her psychology of possibility and introducing my mother and stepfather. Both are 100 percent relevant for this book.

If you open your mind to the assertion that your personal connections affect your health and ability to heal, then you have stepped into the psychology of possibility. In this realm, your health and longevity are affected not only by what you do, but also what you think and feel—with *feeling* taking the lead.

Ellen's other contribution is equally significant because both my mother and stepfather survived—and have thrived—after potentially catastrophic health events. Yes, they had good and prompt medical care, but that only addresses a portion of the "survival" aspect. Really pulling through cancer and a so-called widowmaker heart attack and then regaining vibrant health illustrates the healing power of a loving relationship.

I know what a loving relationship is and I know what it isn't, because I've had both. Like most of the human race, I grew up in a family that was occasionally dysfunctional. (Understand that I was "avoidant dismissive" as a child.) Much to their credit, they gave me a feel for love. As an adult, two failed marriages preceded the secure, happy connection I now enjoy. How do you know when it's "right?"

You feel it first, and then you know it. (This is another discussion in the book—scientifically explained.) Finally, I'm not a perfect mother. Just ask my children. But then, the paradox of being a perfect parent is that a better one is actually the "good enough" mom or dad. Our ability to connect securely with another human being requires that we stumble and fall sometimes.

These facts of my personal life are part of my professional credentials. My own desire to feel deeply connected with people, to thrive within loving relationships, is part of what has energized my calling to help others as a therapist. Those credentials fit in the context of an education that culminated in my training under Susan Johnson, originator of Emotionally-Focused Therapy. Her wisdom centers on the healing power of emotions; it colors the pages of this book. Sue gave our community an academic and clinical grasp of what we knew intuitively but hadn't yet articulated. It's also important to note that I approach the topics in this book with both of my feet planted in systems theory. Thanks to Karl Ludwig Von Bertalanffy and his work in systems theory, Marriage and Family Therapy evolved as one of many disciplines premised on the concept of interconnectedness. In the context of my work, that means the interconnectedness of human beings. We affect each other energetically; there's no escaping that reality, so let's see it as a grand opportunity. We can sum up that opportunity by saying, "The whole is greater than the sum of its parts."

And here's where the ideas for this book began coming together: my radio show. Since 2010, week after week I have interviewed neuroscientists, psychiatrists, cardiologists, psychologists, social workers and many other recognized experts about the topic of "keeping connected," which is the name of my show. Each one seemed to bring a different, yet complementary piece to the giant puzzle of "human relationships." They brought me the science concerning not only how we form deep interpersonal connections, but also the science of why we must form them. Each one enriched my understanding of human biology and behavior and, most particularly, the provable link between the state of our health and the health of our relationships. Correlating the research, I felt confident saying, "We don't have a choice about relationships. It's a matter of love or die."

What I've learned is the substance of this book, as well as an integral part of the process I take couples through in therapy. When I ask them to tell me where they feel anxiety and they think that's a stupid question, I explain the science of why I'm asking the question and why the answer is a marker on the path to healing their relationships.

Most importantly, I am supported by a deeply loving and committed family without which none of this would be possible. My massively attuned husband, Vinny, keeps me sane, makes me laugh and pushes me to be me. He has urged me to take risks and to relish the moment and believe in myself and my message. Vinny is my safe haven and I love him!

A big thanks goes out to my children, I am so proud of you! To Olivia who keeps me honest, to Duncan who keeps me chuckling, to Eva who is a shining light, to Michelle who is fierce and focused and to Spencer who has a wry sense of humor. My children fill me with joy and endless love.

Thank you to my mom, Fredi, and my step dad, Howard, who are my guiding beacons. Smart, loving and generous, thank you thank you thank you for being there for me!

Thank you to my dazzling sisters, Devin, Michon and Cavan. You all showed me possibility, courage and persistence. I feel influenced and moved by your wise words, your loving support and all of your creative pursuits. You taught me to never, never, never give up!

My step brothers and their fabulous wives have been important to my growth and my development, intellectually and emotionally.

I am indebted to the great minds that developed and contributed to the discipline of Marriage and Family Therapy and psychotherapy. There are many, including John Bowlby, Virginia Satir, Sue Johnson and Diana Fosha, to name just a few.

And special thanks to Donna Laikind who influenced me to become a therapist!

I am indebted to my clients who have honored me with sharing their stories and letting me into their inner worlds. You have taught me so much and I only hope that I have helped you in some way.

Other strong influencers in my life include my yoga teacher Gail Cohen, my colleagues Marion Green, Mary and Parker Stacy, the Reverend Paul Whitmore, my dear friends Chris Gould and Gina Ludlow and Susan Fales-Hill who made writing books look graceful. (Which it is not!) You all supported me and gave me the courage and curiosity to forge ahead.

Last and certainly not least, my co-author, Maryann Karinch, who is brilliant, loving and understanding. Thank you for embracing my idea and creating the beautiful and connected words to express it!

—Trevor Crow

Thanks first to Trevor, who has been a joy to work with and an inspiration throughout the process! I offer hugs and appreciation to my family and friends who provide consistent and loving support, specifically Jim McCormick, my Mom, and my brother Karl.

Among the many experts in my life, three who have been particularly important in the development of this work are John Biever, Dan Hughes, and Saroj Parida. You have all taught me so much about the link between healthy interpersonal relationships and healthy minds and bodies. Thank you also to Jim Coan and Sue Johnson, who were most generous in contributing their insights and time. We will continue to benefit from your pioneering work for generations to come.

With great appreciation, I also want to acknowledge Joan Dunphy, our editor and one of the most important mentors in my career, and the wonderful team at New Horizon Press that includes JoAnne Thomas, Caroline Russomanno and Charley Nasta, who designed the wonderful cover.

—Maryann Karinch

Bibliography

Damasio, Antonio. *Descartes' Error: Emotion, Reason, and the Human Brain*. New York: Penguin, 2005.

Fosha, Diana, Daniel J. Siegel, and Marion F. Solomon, eds. *The Healing Power of Emotion: Affective Neuroscience, Development & Clinical Practice*. New York: W.W. Norton, 2009.

Gray, Jeffrey A. *The Psychology of Fear and Stress, 2nd Ed*. Cambridge: Cambridge University Press, 1988.

Hartley, Gregory, and Maryann Karinch. *I Can Read You Like a Book*. Franklin Hills: Career Press, 2007.

Hughes, Daniel. *Building the Bonds of Attachment: Awakening Love in Deeply Troubled Children*. Lanham: Jason Aronson, 2006.

Johnson, Susan. *Hold Me Tight: Your Guide to the Most Successful Approach to Building Loving Relationships*. London: Piatkus Books, 2011.

Langer, Ellen J. *Counterclockwise: Mindful Health and the Power of Possibility*. New York: Ballantine Books, 2009.

Orenstein, Peggy. *Cinderella Ate My Daughter: Dispatches from the Front Lines of the New Girlie-Girl Culture*. New York: Harper, 2011.

Patterson, Paul H. *Infectious Behavior: Brain-Immune Connections in Autism, Schizophrenia, and Depression*. Cambridge: MIT Press, 2011.

Steinbaum, Suzanne. *Dr. Suzanne Steinbaum's Heart Book*. New York: Avery/Penguin, 2013.

Notes

CHAPTER 1

1. Diane Ackerman, "The Brain on Love," *The New York Times*, March 24, 2012. http://opinionator.blogs.nytimes.com/2012/03/24/the-brain-on-love/.
2. Edward Tronick, L.B. Adamson, H. Als and T.B. Brazelton, "Infant emotions in normal and perturbed interactions," Paper presented at the biennial meeting of the Society for Research in Child Development, Denver, CO, (April 1975).
3. "Still Face Experiment: Dr. Edward Tronick," Uploaded on November 30, 2009. http://www.youtube.com/watch?v=apzXGEbZht0.
4. K.M. Gudsnuk and F.A. Champagne, "Epigenetic effects of early developmental experiences." *Clinics in Perinatology*. Vol. 38 (4) (December 2011): 703-17.
5. Ibid.
6. John Bowlby, *Attachment and Loss: Volume 1: Attachment*. (London: The Hogarth Press and the Institute of Psycho-Analysis, 1969), xii.
7. Ibid.
8. M. Ainsworth, M. Blehar, E. Waters, and S. Wall. *Patterns of Attachment*. (Hillsdale, NJ: Erlbaum, 1978).
9. M. Main and J. Solomon, "Discovery of a new, insecure-disorganized/disoriented attachment pattern. (1986) In T. B. Brazelton & M. Yogman (Eds), *Affective development in infancy*, pp. 95-124 (Norwood, New Jersey).

10. C. Hazen, and P. Shaver, "Romantic love conceptualized as an attachment process." *Journal of Personality and Social Psychology*, Vol 52(3), March 1987, 511-524.

11. Walter Isaacson, *Steve Jobs* (Simon & Schuster, 2011).

12. D. Kim Burnham, Ph.D., *The Healing Tribes* (working title; book under development), 2013.

13. Tara Parker-Pope, "What Are Friends For? A Longer Life," *The New York Times*, April 20, 2009.

14. Suzanne Steinbaum, *Dr. Suzanne Steinbaum's Heart Book*, (Avery/ Penguin, 2013), 79.

15. Sudden Cardiac Arrest Association; http://www.suddencardiacarrest. org/aws/SCAA/pt/sd/news_article/55522/_self/layout_details/false.

16. Geoff MacDonald and Mark R. Leary, "Why Does Social Exclusion Hurt? The Relationship Between Social and Physical Pain," *Psychological Bulletin*, American Psychological Association, 2005, Vol 131, No. 2, 202-223.

17. Tara Parker-Pope, "Is Marriage Good for your Health?" *The New York Times*, April 14, 2010.

18. J.E. Graham, L.M. Christina and J.K. Kiecolt-Glaser, "Marriage, health, and immune function: A review of key finding and the role of depression," S. Beach & M. Wamboldt (eds.), *Relational Processes in Mental Health*, Vol 11, American Psychiatric Publishing, Inc., 2006.

19. Craig LeMoult, "Out-Of-Towners Converge On Newtown," NPR, December 20, 2012, http://www.npr.org/2012/12/20/167677284/out -of-towners-converge-on-newtown-conn.

20. From a December 28, 2012, interview with Dr. Daniel Hughes conducted in Annville, PA at his office.

21. Carina Storrs, "Marriage helps survival after heart surgery," *CNNHealth .com*, August 22, 2011, http://www.cnn.com/2011/HEALTH/08/22/ marriage.heart.surgery/index.html.

22. Paul H. Patterson, *Infectious Behavior: Brain-Immune Connections in Autism, Schizophrenia, and Depression.* (The MIT Press, 2011), 3.

CHAPTER 2

1. Daniel J. Siegel, "Emotion as Integration: A Possible Answer to the Question, What is Emotion?" *The Healing Power of Emotion: Affective Neuroscience, Development & Clinical Practice* (W.W. Norton, 2009), 148-149.

2. "Dem Dry Bones" (author unknown) lyrics are inspired by *Ezekiel* 37:1-14, where the prophet visits the "Valley of Dry Bones" and can be found on multiple websites including http://www.kididdles.com/lyrics/d009.html.

3. Gregory Hartley and Maryann Karinch, *I Can Read You Like a Book*, (Career Press, 2007), 188.

4. Jeremy D. Safran, Leslie S. Greenberg (Eds), *Emotion, Psychotherapy & Change* (The Guilford Press, 1991), 3.

5. Ibid, 20.

6. AEDP Institute, "Our Mission," http://www.aedpinstitute.org/about-aedp/mission/.

7. From an interview conducted by David Van Nuys, Ph.D. on Seven Counties Services, Inc. http://www.sevencounties.org/poc/view_doc.php?type=doc&id=44200.

8. Anahad O'Connor, "Really? Constant Stress Makes You Sick," *The New York Times*, April 9, 2012; http://well.blogs.nytimes.com/2012/04/09/really-the-claim-constant-stress-makes-you-sick/.

9. Susan M. Johnson, EdD, *Emotionally Focused Couple Therapy with Trauma Survivors: Strengthening Attachment Bonds* (The Guilford Press, 2005), 179.

10. Mario Mikulincer and Philip R. Shaver, "An attachment perspective on psychopathology," *World Psychiatry*, v.11(1); February 2012; PMC3266769; http://www.ncbi.nlm.nih.gov/pmc/articles/PMC3266769/.

11. NACBT Online Headquarters, "Cognitive Behavioral Therapy," http://www.nacbt.org/whatiscbt.htm.

12. Antonio Damasio, *Descartes' Error: Emotion, Reason, and the Human Brain* (Penguin, 2005).

13. René Descartes, Discourse on the Method of Rightly Conducting One's Reason and of Seeking Truth in the Sciences, 1637; original phrase is listed as "cogito ergo sum," found in Part IV, Section 7 of the work entitled "Principles of Philosophy."

14. Allan N. Schore, "Right-Brain Affect Regulation," *The Healing Power of Emotion* (W.W. Norton & Company, 2009), 112-144.

15. T. Bengtsson and G. Broström, "Famines and mortality crises in 18th and 19th century southern Sweden," (1989) *Genus*, LXVII (No. 2), 119-130.

16. "About the Human Genome Project: What is the Human Genome Project," The Human Genome Management Information System (HGMIS). 2011-07-18. Retrieved 2011-09-02.

17. D. Francis, J. Diorio, D. Liu and M.J. Meaney, "Nongenomic transmission across generations of maternal behavior and stress responses in the rat" *Science* 286 (5442) (November 5, 1999): 1155-8.

18. Michael Kobor, "Childhood Poverty, Stress Shape Genes and Immune System" Scicasts / Epigenomics, October 18, 2012; http://scicasts. com/gene/2031-epigenomics/4937-childhood-poverty-stress-shape -genes-and-immune-system.

19. Ibid.

20. "DNA Methylation—What is DNA Methylation?" January 9, 2013 http://www.news-medical.net/health/DNA-Methylation-What-is -DNA-Methylation.aspx.

21. "Childhood trauma can leave permanent epigenetic marks on DNA," December 3, 2012 http://www.news-medical.net/news/20121203/ Childhood-trauma-can-leave-permanent-epigenetic-marks-on-DNA. aspx.

22. Paul H. Patterson, *Infectious Behavior: Brain-Immune connections in Autism, Schizophrenia, and Depression,* (The MIT Press, 2011), 52.

23. Ibid.

24. Dawson Church, *The Genie in Your Genes*, Energy Psychology Press; Second Edition (2009).

25. James D. Baird, Laurie Nadel, and Bruce Lipton, *Happiness Genes: Unlock the Positive Potential Hidden in your DNA* (New Page Books, 2010).

26. Ibid, Burnham.

27. Ariel Gore, "Epigenetics, Save Me From My Family!" Psychology Today, March 13, 2011; http://www.psychologytoday.com/blog/women -and-happiness/201103/epigenetics-save-me-my-family.

28. Ibid.

29. D. Francis, J Diorio, D. Liu, and M.J. Meaney, Ibid.

CHAPTER 3

1. Walter B Cannon, *Bodily Changes in Pain, Hunger, Fear and Rage: An Account of Recent Research Into the Function of Emotional Excitement*, 2nd ed. New York (Appleton-Century-Crofts, 1929).

2. Jeffrey A Gray, *The Psychology of Fear and Stress, 2nd ed. Cambridge* (Cambridge University Press, 1988).

3. Ibid.

4. Gregory Hartley and Maryann Karinch, *How to Spot a Liar*, First Edition (Career Press, 2005) 27.

5. Ibid.

6. Ibid, p. 28.

7. Stephen W. Porges, "Reciprocal Influences Between Body and Brain in the Perception and Expression of Affect: A Polyvagal Perspective," *The Healing Power of Emotion: Affective Neuroscience, Development & Clinical Practice* (W.W Norton, 2009) 40.

8. Stephen W. Porges in an interview with David Van Nuys, Ph.D., "The Polyvagal Theory with Stephen Porges, Ph.D.", Shrink Rap Radio, June 3, 2011; http://www.shrinkrapradio.com/2011/06/03/265 -%E2%80%93-the-polyvagal-theory-with-stephen-porges-ph-d/

9. John P. Capitanio, Sally P. Mendoza, and Steve W. Cole, "Nervous temperament in infant monkeys is associated with reduced sensitivity of leukocytes to cortisol's influence on trafficking," *Brain, Behavior, and Immunity* Volume 25, Issue 1, January 2011, Pages 151–159; http:// www.sciencedirect.com/science/article/pii/S0889159110004666

10. Paul H. Patterson, *Infectious Behavior: Brain-Immune Connections in Autism, Schizophrenia, and Depression* (The MIT Press, 2011) 25.

11. Ibid, 26.

12. Ibid, 27.

13. Hari Shanker Sharma, Aruna Sharma, "Breakdown Barrier in Stress Alters Cognitive Dysfunction and Induced Brain Pathology: New Perspectives for Neuroprotective Strategies," Michael S. Ritsner (Ed), *Brain Protection in Schizophrenia, Mood, and Cognitive Disorders* (Springer, 2010) 243.

14. Judith Orloff, M.D. "The Ecstasy of Surrender," TEDx; http://www.drjudithorloff.com/.

15. Ibid.

16. Joseph Ledoux, "Searching the Brain for the Roots of fear," *The New York Times*, January 22, 2012; http://opinionator.blogs.nytimes.com/2012/01/22/anatomy-of-fear/.

17. *Report of the National School Shield Task Force*, National Rifle Association; http://www.nraschoolshield.com/NSS_Final_FULL.pdf.

18. John Biever and Maryann Karinch, *The Wandering Mind* (Rowman & Littlefield, 2012).

19. Ibid.

20. Ibid.

21. Ibid.

22. Erin Gersley, "Phobias: Causes and Treatments," November 17, 2001, *AllPsych Journal*; http://allpsych.com/journal/phobias.html

23. Joseph Wolpe and Arnold Lazarus, *Behavior Therapy Techniques*, (Oxford: Pergamon Press Ltd., 1996), 55-56.

24. Ibid, Gernsley.

25. Allan N. Schore, "Attachment and the regulation of the right brain," Attachment & Human Development, Vol. 2, No. 1, (April 2000) 34.

26. Ibid.

27. Daniel Siegel on the Triangle of Well-Being, http://www.youtube.com/watch?v=BGYUbc73JwY.

28. Ibid, Siegel.

29. Ibid.

30. Ibid.

CHAPTER 4

1. The World's 100 Most Influential People: 2012, *TIME* magazine; http://www.time.com/time/specials/packages/completelist/ 0,29569,2111975,00.html.

2. Sam Sommers, *Situations Matter: Understanding How Context Transforms Your World (Riverhead Trade, 2012).*

2. David Brooks, "The Heart Grows Smarter," *The New York Times*, November 5, 2012.

2. Ibid.

3. Gail Collins, "Ohio Gets the Love," *The New York Times*, September 26, 2012.

4. Carina Storrs, "Marriage helps survival after heart surgery," Health .com, CNN, August 22, 2011; http://www.cnn.com/2011/HEALTH/ 08/22/marriage.heart.surgery/index.html.

5. Jeffrey M. Fish, Ph.D., "Are American Friendships Superficial?" *Psychology Today*, September 7, 2010.

6. Peggy Orenstein, "Saving our Daughters from an Army of Princesses," *All Things Considered*, National Public Radio; http://www .npr.org/2011/02/05/133471639/saving-our-daughters-from-an -army-of-princesses.

7. Peggy Orenstein, *Cinderella Ate My Daughter: Dispatches from the Front Lines of the New Girlie-Girl Culture*, (Harper, 2011) 2.

8. Robin H. Pugh Yi and Craig T. Dearfield, "The Status of Women in the U.S. Media 2012," Women's Media Center, 2012, http://wmc.3cdn.net/ a6b2dc282c824e903a_arm6b0hk8.pdf.

9. http://www.investopedia.com/terms/m/mancession.asp#axzz2 INEz7CnU.

10. National Center for Education Statistics, "Fast Facts."

11. Pornography Statistics, Family Safe Media, http://www.family safemedia.com/pornography_statistics.html.

12. "Home porn gives industry the blues," guardian.co.uk, December 16, 2007; http://www.theguardian.com/world/2007/dec/16/film.usa.

13. http://en.wikipedia.org/wiki/National_Science_Foundation.

14. http://en.wikipedia.org/wiki/Centers_for_Disease_Control.

15. "Porn and Relationships: Men's Pornography Use Tied to Lower Self-Esteem in Female Partners;" http://www.huffingtonpost.com/2012/06/01/porn-relationships-men-female-partner-self-esteem_n_1562821.html.

16. Stephanie Pappas, "Is Porn Bad for You?" LiveScience, March 23, 2012; http://www.livescience.com/19251-pornography-effects-santorum.html.

17. Susan Krauss Whitbourne, "An Inside Look at Sexual Fantasies," *Psychology Today*, January 15, 2013.

18. Rich Tosches, "Eulogy for an elk in Boulder," *Denver Post*, January 13, 2013, 5D.

19. Kat Giantis, "Undressed 2012: The Year (so far) in Celebrity Fashion Faux Pax"; http://wonderwall.msn.com/movies/undressed-the-year-so-far-in-celebrity-fashion-faux-pas-21006.gallery#!wallState=0__%2Fmovies%2Fundressed-the-year-so-far-in-celebrity-fashion-faux-pas-21006.gallery%3FphotoId%3D77929.

20. http://digitallife.today.com/_news/2012/09/28/14125511-reddit-user-insults-sikh-woman-over-facial-hair-response-inspires-apology?lite.

21. "National Cathedral Hopes to Set Example By Performing Same-Sex Marriages," *All Things Considered*, National Public Radio, January 9, 2013; http://www.npr.org/2013/01/09/168983534/national-cathedral-hopes-to-set-example-by-performing-same-sex-marriages.

22. http://hq.nolabels.org/page/s/fightingfixing_gs.

CHAPTER 5

1. Paul Grondahl, "Sisters were Sisters, inseparable to the end," *Times Union*, January 23, 2013.

2. Daniel A. Hughes, Ph.D., *Building the Bonds of Attachment: Awakening Love in Deeply Troubled Children* (Jason Aronson Inc, 2006) 299-300.

3. Ibid.

4. Ibid.

5. Ibid.

6. From an e-mail from Saroj Parida, January 29, 2013.

7. "Mindfulness Meditation Research Findings," compiled by Philippe Goldin for Stanford University Department of Psychology, January 2001, 1.

8. Claire Bates, "Is this the world's happiest man? Brain scans reveal French monk has 'abnormally large capacity' for joy—thanks to meditation," *Daily Mail*, October 31, 2012; http://www.dailymail.co.uk/health/article-2225634/Is-worlds-happiest-man-Brain-scans-reveal-French-monk-abnormally-large-capacity-joy-meditation.html.

9. A.B. Newburg and E.G. d'Aquili, "The Neuropsychology of Religious and Spiritual Experience," Journal of Consciousness Studies 7, nos. 11-12 (November-December 2000), 251-266.

10. Ibid, Bates.

11. The Bowen Theory website, http://www.thebowencenter.org/pages/conceptds.html.

CHAPTER 6

1. http://www.merriam-webster.com/dictionary/love.

2. "Hidden secret to success: vulnerability." *USA Weekend*, October 19-21, 2012, 4

3. Ibid.

4. Hakuri Murakami, Norwegian Wood, Vintage Mti edition, 2012

5. Arthur Aron and Bianca Acevedo, "Neural correlates of long-term intense romantic love," *Social Cognitive and Affective Neuroscience*, 2010.

6. Ibid.

7. Ibid.

8. Diana Fosha, Daniel J. Siegel, Marion F. Solomon (Eds),*The Healing Power of Emotion*, (W.W. Norton, 2009) contains articles by Siegel and Schorr.

9. Diane Ackerman, "The Brain on Love," *The New York Times*, March 24, 2012; http://opinionator.blogs.nytimes.com/2012/03/24/the-brain-on-love/.

10. James A. Coan, "Toward a Neuroscience of Attachment," *Handbook of Attachment: Theory, Research, and Clinical Implications* (2nd Edition), edited by Jude Cassidy and Philip R. Shaver (The Guildford Press), 260.

11. From an interview with James A. Coan, January 28, 2013.

12. Ibid.

13. Ibid.

14. Michael W. Kraus, Cassy Huang, and Dachler Keltner, "Tactile Communication, Cooperation, and Performance: An Ethological Study of the NBA," *Emotion* (the peer-reviewed journal), Volume 10, 745-749.

15. Robert I. Sutton, "When NBA Players Touch Teammates More, They Win More," *Psychology Today*, December 21, 2010; http://www.psychologytoday.com/blog/work-matters/201012/when-nba-players-touch-teammates-more-they-win-more.

16. Suzanne Steinbaum, M.D.., D.O., *Dr. Suzanne Steinbaum's Heart Book* (Avery/Penguin USA, 2013) 71-72.

17. From an interview with James A. Coan, January 28, 2013.

18. Ibid.

19. Ibid.

20. Ibid.

21. Ibid.

22. Sue Johnson, *Hold Me Tight* (Little, Brown & Company, 2008).

CHAPTER 7

1. Season 2, Episode 12: "La Douleur Exquise!" of *Sex and the City*

2. Susan Johnson, JA Makinen, and JWMillikin, "Attachment injuries in couple relationships: a new perspective on impasses in couples therapy," *Journal of Marital and Family Therapy*, 2001 Apr;27(2):145-55

3. Greg Hartley and Maryann Karinch, *Date Decoder* (Adams Media, 2008) 180-182.

4. Ibid.

5. Rhonda Schwartz, Brian Ross and Chris Francescani, "Edwards Admits Sexual Affair; Lied as Presidential Candidate," (*ABC News*: August 8, 2008), http://abcnews.go.com/Blotter/story?id=5441195#

.UZULgcoOF80; Justin Elliott, "The truth about Newt and his cancer-stricken wife," (*Salon:* March 8, 2011), http://www.salon .com/2011/03/08/gingrich_divorce_hospital_cancer/.

6. The character Harry Goldblatt appeared throughout seasons 5 and 6 of *Sex and the City*.

CHAPTER 8

1. Brené Brown, "The power of vulnerability," TEDtalks, Uploaded on January 3, 2011 http://www.youtube.com/watch?v=iCvmsMzlF7o.

2. Y. Takezako, Y. Kanda, C. Arai, N. Takezako, Y. Shirai, N. Hirano, A. Miwa, A.Togawa, "Spontaneous remission in acute type adult T-cell leukemia/lymphoma," *Journal Leukemia & Lymphoma*, September 2000.

3. H.Kappauf, WM Gallmeier, PH Wünsch, HO Mittelmeier, J Birkmann, G Büschel, G Kaiser, J Kraus, "Complete spontaneous remission in a patient with metastatic non-small-cell lung cancer. Case report, review of the literature, and discussion of possible biological pathways involved.," *Annals of Oncology*, 1997 Oct, 8:10, 1031-9.

4. EFLewison, "Spontaneous regression of breast cancer," *National Cancer Institute Monograph*, 1976 Nov, 44:, 23-6.

5. Jeanne Lenzer, "The Body Can Beat Terminal Cancer—Sometimes," *Discover*, September 2007; http://discovermagazine.com/2007/sep/ the-body-can-stave-off-terminal-cancer-sometimes.

6. Ibid.

7. Ibid.

CHAPTER 9

1. Christian Jarrett, Ph.D., "Mirror Neurons: The Most Hyped Concept in Neuroscience?" *Psychology Today*, December 10, 2012; http://www .psychologytoday.com/blog/brain-myths/201212/mirror-neurons -the-most-hyped-concept-in-neuroscience.

2. Giacomo Rizzolatti and Laila Craighero, "The Mirror-Neuron System," *Annual Review of Neuroscience*, 2004, 27:169-92; http://www.kuleuven.be/mirrorneuronsystem/readinglist/Rizzolatti%20&%20Craighero%202004%20-%20The%20MNS%20-%20ARN.pdf.

3. Ibid.

4. Ibid.

5. Lee Siegel, "The Book of Self-Love—Narcissism," *The New York Times*, February 5, 2010; http://www.nytimes.com/2010/02/07/books/review/Siegel-t.html?pagewanted=all&_r=0.

6. Kristin Neff, "The Space Between Self-Esteem and Self Compassion," TEDx; http://www.self-compassion.org.

7. From an interview with James A. Coan, Ph.D. on January 28, 2013.

8. Ibid.

9. Ibid.

10. Ibid.

11. Ibid.

12. *Star Trek*, Season 3, Episode #67.

13. Paul Ekman, *Emotions Revealed, Second Edition: Recognizing Faces and Feelings to Improve Communication and Emotional Life* (Holt Paperbacks, Second Edition, 2007).

14. Hillel Aviezer, Yaacov Trope, Alexander Todorov, "Body cues, Not Facial Expressions, Discriminate Between Intense Positive and Negative Emotions," *Science Magazine*, November 30, 2012, Vol. 338 no. 6111, 1225-1229; http://www.sciencemag.org/content/338/6111/1225.abstract.

15. Ibid.

16. Ibid.

17. J. M Gottman, K. McCoy, J. Coan, and H. Collier, "The Specific Affect Coding System (SPAFF) for observing emotional communication in marital and family interaction," (Mahwah, NJ: Erlbaum, 1995) 3.

18. Ibid.

19. J. Coan and J.M. Gottman, "The Specific Affect Coding System (SPAFF)," *Handbook of Emotion Elicitation and Assessment* (Oxford University Press, 2007) 272.

20. Ibid.

21. Jim McCormick, Loren B. Belker, and Gary S. Topchik, *The First-Time Manager*, Sixth Edition (AMACOM Books, 2012) 199.

22. Paul Freedman and Ken Goldstein, "Measuring Media Exposure and the Effects of Negative Campaign Ads," *American Journal of Political Science*, Vol. 43, No. 4 (Oct., 1999), 1189-1208; Midwest Political Science Association.

23. Margaret Shih, Todd L. Pittinsky, and Nalini Ambady, "Stereotype Susceptibility: Identity Salience and Shifts in Quantitative Performance," *Psychological Science*, January 1999, Vol. 10 no. 1, 80-83.

24. Ibid.

25. Paul M. Lefcourt, *Locus of Control* (John Wiley & Sons, 1976).

26. Ellen J. Langer, *Counterclockwise: Mindful Health and the Power of Possibility* (Ballantine Books, 2009) 98.

27. Ibid, 99.

28. Ibid.

29. Gregory Hartley and Maryann Karinch, *I Can Read You Like a Book* (Career Press, 2007).

30. Ibid, 130.

31. "Stress by Generation: Stress at any age is still stress," American Psychological Association, summary of 2013 study http://www.apa .org/news/press/releases/stress/2012/generations.aspx.

32. From a conversation with David M. Reiss, March 3, 2013.

33. Daniel J. Siegel, recorded lecture "The Triangle of Well-Being," October 2010; http://greatergood.berkeley.edu/gg_live/science _meaningful_life_videos/speaker/daniel_siegel/the_triangle_of _wellbeing/.

34. Ibid.

35. Ibid.

36. Ibid.

37. Ibid.